TACKING THROUGH LIFE

CAROLYN WASIK

Thank You Longwood Library with Special Thanks to Anthony and Alyssa for their Technical Support —

Carolyn Wasik

SisterShip
women on the water

Published in Australia in 2020 by SisterShip Press Pty Ltd

Part of SisterShip Magazine and SisterShip Training NSW, Australia

www.sistershippress.com

Printed and bound in Australia by SisterShip Press Pty Ltd

Edited by Ann Leander

National Library of Australia data:

SisterShip Press Pty Ltd, 2020, Tacking Through Life

Paperback ISBN: 978-0-6487833-0-5

Ebook ISBN: 978-0-6487833-1-2

Large Print ISBN: 978-0-6487833-7-4

In collaboration with SisterShip Magazine and SisterShip Training

www.sistershippress.com

www.sistershipmagazine.com

www.sistershiptraining.com

Dedicated to Gert and Maggie May

I would like to express my appreciation to Ann Leander, Editor, who worked with me through this past year and still maintained an upbeat attitude. I am sure she grew a few grey hairs but she was tireless. Thank you, Ann. And to SisterShip Press, founders Jackie Parry and Shelley Wright. I thank them for seeing something in this story that might warrant being published. They both added a personal positive touch in their communications which kept me going. I'm certain that working with a novice like me must be frustrating at times. I'm also impressed that Jackie just completed the Melbourne to Hobart Yacht Race, making history as one of the first all-female, two-handed crew. Congratulations.

And my very personal thank you to Vivian my sister and John Boyd her husband. They opened their home and hearts to my Maggie May, my golden retriever. Maggie May died while I was away. There are no words for that.

Peace, Carolyn

CONTENTS

worked, I made sketches to pass the time. I could just imagine what the neighbors were thinking of these nocturnal activities.

After work the next day we drove back to City Island in the MG with the oak still in the jigs. The boatyard workers scratched their heads and looked on as if we were crazy. Thinking back, they might have been right. Gert removed the ribs from the jig and fastened them to the inside of the boat hull. He even doubled up on some of the ribs. When I asked why, he mumbled something that sounded like 'rough seas' and 'pounding'. Surely I was hearing him wrong. Then he painted the undersides blue with the fungus prevention paint, so highly toxic it caught in his throat, but he didn't seem to mind.

Our weekends, for half a year, were spent painting and cleaning to get that boat ready. I was still teaching, and our progress had become the Monday morning entertainment in the teachers' lounge. But hard physical work has never bothered me; I guess that comes from growing up on a farm. Besides, at the end of the day we would always find some quaint seafood restaurant on City Island. Seafood and champagne are my basic food and drink needs.

The day finally came when, freshly painted white, the boat was ready to be launched. She was fitted with a one cylinder Volvo engine, rebuilt by Gert. There were times, going through 'cuts' in the Bahamas, when I thought my hair dryer had more power than that engine. We christened the boat *Hasard*, a Danish word that meant, loosely translated, betting with more than you had in your hand. In short, gambling. Gamble sounded about right to me as so much of what we had both done in our lives so far had been a tad risky. Someone once said he thought we "walked on the dark side of the moon". Yes, *Hasard* was a good name.

Finally, after ten years on dry dock, *Hasard* was lowered – ever so gently – into the water. At last she was floating, and she looked beautiful. We spent our first night on board watching her settle in, and noticing how her wood was soaking in the sea water. This was to be expected in a boat that had been on dry dock for so long and anyway, "That's what bilge pumps are for," Gert said. As I sat ankle deep in water I was convinced we were sinking, but Gert explained the wood just needed to swell. The next day, most of the water had gone – the bilge pump had done its job. The tide was high and off we sailed for our home port, Mount Sinai on the north shore of Long Island.

We had a great year; sailing in the Great South Bay on the south shore of Long Island. Summers are the best time of year there, with warm weather and almost always an afternoon breeze from the southwest to blow us homewards. We usually sailed to Fire Island from the south shore of Long Island where we would anchor out and walk across the dunes. The sandy beaches extended to the Atlantic Ocean, which on some days was as blue and warm as the Caribbean.

During the winter months, our imaginations started working overtime. Long Island can be colder than most think and the freezing snow and wet slush make driving anywhere miserable. All we could think about were warm, tropical islands. This is when we started seriously considering this living on a boat idea, "She's a strong vessel," Gert said. "We could rent our house and take off on *Hasard* and see where she takes us."

Gert always said he wanted to sail around the world but I hadn't taken him too seriously. My art projects of dying and painting on fabric were going at that time. I had even been commissioned to make cloth for an entire wedding party. Yes, I too had dreamed of traveling around the world but never really given much thought to how I would do this. It doesn't hurt to dream.

But now we talked seriously. Renting out our home, we calculated, would give us enough money to live on while sailing. Gert would always find work as a mechanic, he could work on anything, anywhere. I was still teaching but, impulsive as I am, I finished off the school year and then quit. My biggest regret came years later at pension time. Fifteen years of teaching and I was suddenly out of the system.

So – we had a plan. Kind of.

⌒

That summer, I took a job as a mate on a big motor yacht out of Montauk. The yachting community on the East End of Long Island draws the very wealthy; it is said that almost one third of the entertainment business lives or parties on the East End in the summer. My job paid well, as the owners were extremely wealthy. It was fascinating to see how the other half lives. The yacht was brand new and in reality, I had little to do but shop for exotic foods and serve cocktails. In the meantime. Gert closed his shop and worked out of our barn for a following of devoted car owners. That summer we saved to have enough money to take off for the Bahamas in the fall.

We lived on our boat that winter, as we continued preparing for our trip. *Hasard* needed a lot of equipping just to get off Long Island. I can only compare living on a day sailer boat to camping on water in a van. There was no refrigeration, no toilet, no stove, no running water, and no heat, not to mention instruments like depth sounders, self-steering gear and radios, which, I was later to learn, are quite important on a boat.

We left Long Island late in the season. The weather, we knew, would be unpredictable as the hurricane season was far from over. The night before we left, our friends from my work and Gert's garage came down to the dock to say goodbye. There was a lot of drinking and toasting; everyone was in a celebratory mood but few could believe we really planned to sail this boat to Florida. Years later a friend confessed that her husband had advised her to, "Say a final goodbye as you'll probably never see them alive again."

We sailed the next day and within an hour were engulfed in fog. To me there is nothing more dangerous or scary on the water than poor visibility. We took down the sails and Gert started the motor. Moving along at about three knots I figured it would take days at this rate to reach the East River in Manhattan. I stood on the foredeck peering through the fog, straining my ears to hear other boats. All was eerily quiet but for fog horns.

This was crazy. We were sailing in fog down the middle of the shipping lane of the Long Island Sound where barges and tankers were coming and going between the Atlantic and the East River. Thank God I knew so little about sailing and its dangers. We spent the entire day motoring, slowly and nervously, until later in the afternoon I heard what sounded like an aircraft coming straight for us. I ducked and started screaming to Gert, convinced we would be hit. Suddenly, out of the fog, a motorboat appeared heading directly for us. I screamed louder but at the last minute, just as I was about to jump overboard, the fog lifted and the motorboat swerved. We were still alive.

And then – what could have been more fitting in that fearful afternoon? – there in front of us was the Execution Rocks Lighthouse. It stands on jagged rocks, which rise up in the middle of Long Island Sound between New Rochelle and Sands Point, an infamous serial killer burial ground. I began to wonder. There had been warnings all the way on this trip, but was I reading too much into these signs? Wide eyed, I glanced at Gert but he only laughed. We were at the Nancy Drew mystery part of the story where you say, *Turn around! There's something bad out there!* But, just like Nancy Drew, we shrugged and turned our attention back to sailing.

We anchored for the night in Port Washington. The East River has a strong current and with a boat as small as ours, (with our hair dryer strength engine), we had to wait for the tide to turn or be pushed backwards. We had completed the first leg of our journey and I was happy just to stop moving. I hadn't once asked myself if I had done the right thing; leaving a stable job, giving up our house. This was an adventure, and adventures are not necessarily easy, but I heard the voice of Gert's late father, "Better to get going and have an accident than never to get going at all." A wonderful way to approach life.

Time for dinner. For cooking we had a propane cylinder and a burner that screwed on to the top – a one-burner cooker. I chopped up a bunch of vegetables and tossed them in my new pressure cooker. I had read somewhere in those cruising magazines that this is what you did. I felt nervous. I had never used one before but heard plenty of pressure cooker explosion stories – my own Mom had blown up a few while canning. But my first attempt was a success. I made a soup of sorts that we ended up calling gruel as it looked like something from a Viking story, rough and primitive, all the vegetables kind of smashed together. This dish was to become our staple meal throughout the trip.

That night, huddled in our warm down bedrolls, we laughed about the day. Gert was satisfied with our progress and I, well honestly, I was happy to be alive. I tend to be dramatic, dividing everything into life and death scenarios; if Gert and I ever fought I would look at him and ask, "Well? Are we getting divorced?" Our arguments were never divorce material. We poured two shots of Danish firewater, Aquavit forty-five percent alcohol and ninety percent proof, the obligatory Danish celebration drink, and toasted our 'good health' as we always did. "The rest will be a piece of cake," Gert assured me.

⸎

We took off next morning into the bright October sunshine with light wind from the east, headed for Hell's Gate and New York Harbor. If you've ever taken a boat through this area you will know what a thrill it is to see New York City from this perspective. It's also a little terrifying as the East River is strong. Passing Rikers Island Penitentiary I wondered what was in the inmates' minds as they watched our little sailboat pass by. It might have been the first time they'd felt safer behind bars.

Sailing down the East River and passing by Manhattan is a sight I will never forget. But the greatest thrill is entering New York Harbor. I'm not particularly patriotic but I imagine how my grandparents must have felt, having left their families in a war-torn Europe, a bittersweet taste in their mouths and a heaviness in their hearts, entering this harbor and seeing the Statue of Liberty and the Manhattan skyline. To this day, no matter how many times I return to New York City, I feel a freedom I never experience anywhere else in the world.

THE ATLANTIC OCEAN IS BIG – OUR BOAT IS SMALL – AND I MUST BE CRAZY

My heart raced as we left New York Harbor. The day was crisp and an onshore breeze caught our sails. I looked into the deep dark water. Memories of driving over bridges when I was little were flooding back, but I pushed them away. I needed to concentrate. *Hasard* was entering the wide and scary Atlantic Ocean and I was in charge of watching out for big ships. This was not the cow pond.

What had I got myself into? I waivered somewhere between excited and terrified. There was no turning back: our house was rented and I had quit my job but – most importantly for me – how humiliating would it be to return to Long Island and admit I'd been afraid?

You never knew what to expect from October weather. The wind seemed quite strong to me and again there was that damn fog settling in. This was only day three of our cruising life and I was already having doubts. I looked at Gert at the helm. As always, he wore that grin on his face which set me thinking of those weird sailing stories about psychotic captains and their crew. Gert often said there is only one captain on a boat. I thought it was just another male macho thing. But now, with search for the rule book. I laid on that horn and started waving my arms like a madwoman. The bridge man couldn't mistake the message.

The Atlantic waves were pushing us. Gert was grappling to maintain control of the boat as she flew towards the bridge. This was not an easy maneuver and people on both sides of the inlet looked on with expressions of shock. When the bridge opened just in time, their horror changed to cheering.

We had arrived at Shark River, New Jersey.

I COULD HAVE WALKED AND BEEN HERE SOONER – CAPE MAY, NEW JERSEY

We anchored in the river. Neither of us spoke, the glowers said it all. I went below to pour a drink, mumbling something about not being hungry so if he wanted something to eat he should make it himself. I curled up on my bunk, pretending to sleep.

Drinking our coffee the next morning, we still were not speaking. But someone had to break the silence.

"If you're ready, let's get going," I snapped. I knew I had to go right then or I never would. This was not the moment to debate whether this sailing idea had been smart or not. Gert said nothing. He just stood up and went topsides. As I cleared away the breakfast things, I heard the grinding of the winch as it lifted the anchor.

We motored slowly out of Snake River, back towards the bridge. This time I read the directions on the air horn can and knew the bridge language – two long blasts followed by two short blasts. So simple. The bridge opened and we were back in the Atlantic.

Gert and I never stayed mad very long. We looked at each other and started to laugh. I filled our thermos, because coffee never tastes better than when you're at sea in calm conditions. The sun came out and a gentle breeze followed us. For once there was no fog. In the ocean we raised the sails; next stop Manasquan Inlet.

I went below to check our exact position. Well, kind of exact. I would figure this out eventually and managing a compass was a hell of a lot easier with gentle waves and sunshine.

We didn't have to go far. We entered the inlet without any disasters and motored up the Manasquan River before turning south and entering Point Pleasant Canal which would connect us to our goal, Barnegat Bay. We continued south for three days, winding around marshes and small bays, anchoring every night and leaving early each morning.

As luck would have it, the yacht I had worked on during the summer was to be moved to Palm Beach for the family's winter vacation. "Would I work for them again?" the owner asked. Of course, I would! I was due there soon. There was no time to waste. Sightseeing would have to wait for another time.

As we approached Atlantic City, looking for a place to anchor, we felt a thump. *Hasard* stopped dead in the water.

"Shit!" I said. "What was that?"

"Did you check the chart for water depth?" Gert yelled.

If looking over the side of the boat and thinking you couldn't see bottom was checking the depth, I thought I had, but as I have mentioned, *Hasard* was not equipped with a depth sounder. It was becoming clear to me you have to pay attention to everything with this sailing life. So much for champagne and suntan lotion.

We had run aground outside the Coast Guard Station. A group of men were pointing at us and laughing. "Looks like you got yourself stuck," one of the Officers called out unnecessarily. "How much water do you draw?"

"Three and a half feet," I yelled back. More laughs in the background.

"Uh huh. Looks like you're here for the next few hours.

Tide's out and you're grounded on one of the highest spots in the area."

Gert and I looked at each other, flushed with embarrassment. Gert threw out the anchor. We went below and swallowed a shot of Aquavit – actually two. A family tradition of Gert's dictates you need one for each leg. We spent the next hour or so going over those damn charts. We could so easily have sunk *Hasard*, or run her into something.

It was four in the afternoon. It would be ages before the tide came in to lift us. I made gruel. We played Rummy 500, our usual evening pastime, and settled in for the wait. A few hours later I felt *Hasard* move. We were floating in the dark. We motored away from the Coast Guard Station, anchored closer to Atlantic City, and fell back into bed. At about four in the morning we both jumped up; our engine had started.

"What the Hell!" Gert shouted, springing buck-naked out of his sleeping bag, assuming someone was trying to steal the boat. There was no sign of life, yet the engine was still running. With the aid of a flashlight, Gert fiddled and tweaked then realized what the problem was; a wire had somehow shorted out and jump started the engine. He sorted the problem and we climbed back into our bed to try to get some sleep.

Time was running short now. At daybreak we pulled anchor for a motor ride to Cape May Inlet where we anchored for the night, without anything weird happening for once.

vessel is to the left or right of you by their light configuration. A cargo ship was approaching and it appeared to be heading directly toward us as both red and green lights were visible. I woke Gert.

I could tell by the calmness of his voice that Gert was trying not to alarm me. "Don't change your course," he instructed. "He'll be turning and you'll see his port lights, so we'll pass port to port." I looked doubtful. "Nothing to worry about," he added confidently.

But, just in case, he decided to stay in the cockpit and nodded off again. I kept a wary eye on the cargo ship which I judged to be directly on a collision course with us as I could still see both port and starboard lights. Fifteen minutes went by. *He'll turn at the last minute*, I thought, remembering Gert's words. Despite their size, these big ships can come up quite fast. My anxiety escalated. Finally, panicked, I shook Gert. "Wake up! That ship's right on our nose."

"Hold your course," he said, maddeningly calm. "I'm telling you, he will turn."

But soon it became apparent he was *not* turning. The calm left Gert's voice and he yelled for me to turn to starboard while he fired up the engine. I was shaking and my chest tightened. The motor wasn't starting so Gert leapt below to do whatever he does to convince it to go. The ship was getting closer and closer. I held my breath, my knuckles turned white. At last I heard the motor turn over – we were saved!

I heard something else too – a voice yelling something that sounded a lot like, "*Assholes!*"

Out of danger at last, and heading for the shore, out of the shipping lanes, I exploded.

"Park this thing *now!*" I screamed.

"You don't park a boat!" Gert answered. "And anyway, there's no harbor until we get to the Chesapeake and Delaware Canal."

"I don't care how – just get to land!"

Gert recognized how scared I was. He threw out an anchor

as soon as we sighted land but there was no protection from the waves of the Delaware. *Hasard* bucked like a bronco at a state fair. I had not stopped shaking. The sails were all wadded up on the deck, the waves were still crashing and the boat was filling with water. I went below, my feet sloshing through water. Out on the companionway, I heard Gert projectile vomiting over the side. I guess the combination of a cheese and pepperoni meal earlier in the day and the rocking of *Hasard* on those waves, and maybe, just maybe, a little apprehension about what had just happened, made him nervous.

Neither of us slept that night. This was getting to be a regular occurrence. The bilge pump worked all night but the water in the cabin didn't drop below four or five inches. At daylight we pulled anchor.

I wish I could remember what kept me going those days. Maybe, since I knew how good sailing could be, I figured you just had to take the bad with the good. It seemed, however, we were getting our fair share of the bad.

Over twenty-five thousand ships pass through the Chesapeake and Delaware Canal every year I read, yet surprisingly it turned out to be the easiest part of the trip so far. My fears of drowning ease when I can see dry land and in the next couple of States we would be sailing the narrower parts of the Intracoastal Waterway (ICW). Moreover, the weather would be warmer every day.

The journey through the Chesapeake Bay took us three days. We anchored every night and spent our nights eating, you've guessed it – gruel. And drinking Aquavit, the mandatory two shots that had now, I realized, crept up to four.

At the end of each day, without the self-steering equipment which so many people consider vital, we were both exhausted. We didn't even have a wheel, just a wooden tiller to steer the boat. Remember, *Hasard* was only supposed to be a day sailer in the soft breezes of the sunny, Long Island summers. How long ago those days seemed now.

As we approached the entrance to Norfolk Harbor we saw gigantic ships and military personnel sailing around in dinghies, keeping an eye out for whatever they keep an eye out for. It appeared they were watching out for people like us because, as we gawked at the ships, we apparently sailed too close and a military boat approached us with guns drawn.

Now all became clear. If we had looked at the charts we would have noticed a red half circle indicating a danger zone, prohibiting non-military boats. We made a speedy exit and headed for the next anchorage across the harbor, at the entrance to the famous Great Dismal Swamp.

THE GREAT DISMAL SWAMP – VIRGINIA

In 1728, when George Washington made his first visit to the Swamp, he suggested draining it and dredging a north-to-south canal that would connect the waters of the Chesapeake Bay in Virginia and the Albemarle Sound in North Carolina. Why the name? Because early explorers, the story goes, lived dismally, constantly wet and sleeping on fallen logs and in trees to try to keep dry. The canal would be fed by the waters from Lake Drummond, its brownish color due to the vegetation from the swamp – juniper, cypress, and gum trees which contained tannic acids and prohibited the growth of bacteria. This meant the water stayed fresh for a very long time. People believed it held magical qualities and, if drunk regularly, prevented sickness and promoted longevity. I was tempted to drink it myself; I was hoping to live for a long time.

We would have to motor down this canal which could be boring but after the Delaware crossing I was ready to be bored. This area made me think of this country's history. We were entering the South and if you know your U.S. history, you will not wonder why this country is so divided. I'm not just talking about the geography and the weather. People live at a different pace in the South, everything is slower.

using them this trip – who needed pajamas? I was barely sleeping so into the hole they went.

Luckily for us, the boatyard wasn't too far back. They hauled *Hasard* out of the water while we went to the laundromat to wash our wet clothes and to the store to buy groceries. By six in evening we were back in the water, with the damage repaired, unable to believe our luck.

The rest of the trip to Florida was relatively uneventful. Well, relative in our terms. We anchored in Beaufort, a very pretty town that even had public showers to cater to boaters traveling this north-south route who needed a respite from the Intracoastal. After Beaufort we headed towards Hilton Head, South Carolina. We were getting close to the finish line.

As we approached the marina at Hilton Head, I gaped at the huge yachts. We had heard it was expensive but I was in the mood to splurge. "Let's dock here for the night," I suggested, "and treat ourselves to dinner."

We had finally purchased a used VHF radio, in the Southport marina where we'd had the repairs done. The antenna was already attached and the wires ran inside the mast. It was high time. I felt very sailor-like as I used it to contact the marina.

"What's your length?" The voice sounded pompous, more like a Connecticut lawyer than a dock-master. No southern drawl here with a "howdy ma'am."

"Twenty-eight feet," I told him. No response came for a couple of minutes. I thought I must have broken the radio but then the same voice came back with, "I believe we can find a spot for you near the dinghy dock." We got the message. I figured the dock-master felt he had to be nice to us. After all, we might have been eccentric millionaires.

We showered and dressed for dinner, aware we'd be rubbing

shoulders with the khaki pants and blue blazer crowd. But we didn't care. In the marina restaurant we laughed, ordered a bottle of champagne, and enjoyed the extravagant evening. Of course, we also blew our two-week budget but hey, it was worth it.

The following day, I contacted the captain of the yacht I was to be working on in Palm Beach. The family were due to fly down shortly and the captain, as I expected, was frantic, "Just catch a plane and get down here fast."

We were near Savannah, so we anchored there while I looked for a flight. In the meantime, Gert called our best friend Jimmy who'd been checking in on our house while we were away. He told Gert that our tenants had left two weeks after we had. "Great," Gert had muttered. "Good start."

"But not to worry,' Jimmy added. "I've paid the mortgage for the month so everything's fine." Did I mention he was our best friend?

I called the yacht captain back to inform him of our progress. "Just do what you have to do," he growled. "And don't worry about the fare," he added as an afterthought. "The boat-owner will pay."

⌇

This was the plan. While I was working on the yacht, in Palm Beach Gert would fly back to Long Island, straighten out everything there and get the house rented again.

Surprisingly, everything worked out. Three weeks later we met up again in Savannah. Our home was rented, I'd finished my job on the yacht and we had some cash again.

Life was good.

FLORIDA – AT LAST

We lived and sailed for close to three years, crossing the Gulf Stream and cruising around the Bahama Islands. Despite *Hasard*'s size and lack of instruments, and the occasional near-death experiences, I did enjoy the lifestyle. Yes, living on a sailboat is tough but I've never been considered a fluff.

By the time we reached the Exuma Islands we had run out of money. Neither Gert nor I could imagine quietly giving up sailing, so we made a pact with ourselves: we would continue this cruising life later, in three years or so, but on a larger boat. We were only in our late thirties. We talked of traveling far – a circumnavigation of the world even. There was a lot to think about; how would we support this lifestyle? We would also need a larger boat. We were young – we would make money somehow. Gert would have no problem as he can fix anything mechanical and has never been afraid of hard work. But my teaching job relied on me staying in one place for an extended period of time, which does not lend itself to the cruising life. Plus, I was tired of teaching. I wanted to do something else, but what?

At least we still had a home, a place to live when we returned life raft, safety equipment, a new radio; and that was just the start. Fortunately, we were both making good money which we poured into the boat. I was still working in the psychiatric emergency room, which my friends considered the ideal job for someone as crazy as me. No-one could believe I would leave a stable job with a state pension to go off sailing. Again.

I have been accused of acting without thought. My philosophy has always been, *just do it, everything will work out in the end*. Gert and I used to imagine that if we were down to our last twenty dollars we would go out buy a bottle of champagne and then figure out what to do next. People must have thought we had tons of money but that wasn't the case and still is not. We have always believed that, while we are capable of making money it is better spent on adventures than 'things'. Fine thoughts when you're young and healthy.

Now, where to live while we worked on completing the buying transaction?

A few years back we had built a barn on our property, which was not sold with the house. With a wood-burning stove and a small bathroom it would be comfortable enough for the two months we needed to stay there, even those winter months when the temperature can drop to freezing. We moved our belongings out of the house, piled them onto a boat trailer, pulled it out of one driveway and into another next door which led to the barn. This all had to be done manually as I had just sold one of our two cars and the other one didn't have a tow hitch.

Gert and I had put so much energy into that house. It had been our first home and was sweet with the memories of close to fifteen years. I wiped away a tear and I think Gert did too. Were we doing the right thing? Until this moment I'd been so caught up in the excitement, I had never stopped to think of the 'what ifs?' I looked down at Maggie May. She was walking next to us her tail between her legs and looking backwards towards our home, wondering, I am sure, what the hell we were doing.

We lived in the barn on Long Island that fall and winter

while preparing *Zivio* for our voyage. Temperatures in New York often drop below freezing and we were thankful for the wood burning stove we had installed in the barn. *Zivio* was tied to the dock about twenty minutes away and plugged in space heaters while we worked.

Before we officially took ownership of *Zivio* we arranged a survey, just like buying a house. This was all new to us. We contacted the Wooden Boat Museum in Connecticut and the Wooden Boat magazine and were told they could recommend only one person for an old wooden boat like this. His name was Giffy. He was eighty-two years old and retired but for this boat maybe, just maybe, he would reconsider. He was living in Vermont, but no-one knew for sure how to reach him. We made extensive inquiries and finally tracked him down. We called and told him about the boat and where she was located and he said he would think about it. He called a couple of days later and said yes, he would do it but I would have to pay for a second guy, as he was not climbing up any forty-two foot mast at his age. He said he would go down to the marina in a couple of weeks, write up a report and send it to us. He asked about our plans for this boat and we told him we planned to live on board and circumnavigate the world. A silence followed on the other end of the line. I can only imagine what he was thinking, *Yeah I've heard that one before.*

Three weeks later his report arrived. He deemed *Zivio* more than capable of sailing around the world but added it was unclear, as he was not acquainted with them, what the prospective buyers were capable of. Smart guy.

We negotiated with the owners and the deal was set. We would pick up *Zivio* in a few weeks. Meanwhile we were still living in the unfinished barn, a place we'd never imagined as our living space. We'd set up our bed on the dirt floor. Maggie May, right next to us on her customized dog bed, seemed unbothered by the state of the floor.

A customer of Gert's loved to tell the story of how he had

dropped off his car early one morning. As usual he left instructions for Gert on the tool chest inside the barn about the work he needed. As he slid open the barn door, Gert and I both looked up. The customer couldn't stop laughing. Here he was, bringing his car to be repaired and what does he find? His mechanic and wife in bed.

⌇

Time passed and all paperwork for the sale was finally completed. Over half the money from the sale of the house would be used to buy the boat. The rest would be used to outfit *Zivio* and supplement my meagre pension for cruising.

Since we were still working, we would have to move *Zivio* on the weekend. We kept a careful eye on the weather. The only storm brewing appeared to be off the coast of Florida. We calculated the trip from Maine to our home port of Mount Sinai, Long Island would not take more than a couple of days so that should be fine.

We packed the car and as we pulled out of the driveway, a beat-up truck came screeching around the corner. Out stepped Jim, a big burly Irishman, with his clothes in a pillowcase. Jim was Gert's oldest friend. They had known each other since Gert moved to the United States from Denmark in 1971.

He lifted a case of beer into the back of the car, all he needed for the perfect weekend. He threw his six foot plus frame, beer belly included, next to Maggie May into the back seat of our old Volvo station wagon. He had just left work and obviously taken a shower as his wild grey hair and full beard were still glistening with drops of water. He looked like Jerry Garcia from the Grateful Dead. Maggie nuzzled up close to him.

Loudly, he said – Jim said everything loudly – "Well Maggie, what are they getting us into?" Maggie scratched her ear. Was she wondering the same thing?

After an eight-hour middle of the night drive, we arrived in

Maine sometime before dawn. Following some warming shots of Danish firewater, we all passed out in the car and woke to a foggy Maine morning. We were to meet the owners at ten that morning as they wanted to say their final good-bye to their boat. It had been some time since Gert and I had last seen *Zivio*. I wondered if we would recognize her among the many boats in the marina. We had never seen her tied to a dock – when we were last here she had been floating in the harbor.

Turning a corner, I heard Gert gasp.

Jim's eyes widened. "And you two were going to sail her for the first time without me?"

I swallowed. He had a point. This looked like an awful lot of boat to handle.

We climbed on board. Maggie held back and needed to be lifted.

As I stepped down into *Zivio* I was taken aback by her beauty. It had been a while since we had seen her and now she was ours. She looked so cozy. The inside was finished in mahogany, like an old library, with book shelves just waiting for my books, and a small wine closet. I felt I could smell the rich wood.

The forward cabin had bunks for two people and a tiny toilet and sink, while the rear cabin – the captain's quarters – had a head and even a shower. We felt like kids in a candy shop. We were doing this, we were going to live on this boat!

The owners had left a box of pastries and a coffee pot set up for breakfast. They knew we were getting in late and wanted us to wake from our first night on board with a fresh cup of coffee. They had loved this boat and I understood why. She was like a big comfy armchair in an old library, I had brought candles which I promptly lit and the three of us sat down on the settees. We had that bottle of Aquavit and so began a late evening of toasting the beginning of our new life. This was to be our home. We never thought we would find a boat as beautiful as Zivio at a price we could afford. To us she was everything we wanted, a sturdy wooden boat with a classic interior. Of course, we were not thinking of the maintenance and other expenses on a boat like this; we were two romantics preparing for an adventure of a lifetime.

Maggie stayed in the cockpit. She looked unimpressed.

I turned on the marine radio and tuned into the NOAA weather station. (NOAA, I discovered, stands for National Oceanic Atmospheric Administration). After considerable screeching and beeping, a weather alert came through. Winds were picking up.

I looked anxiously at Gert. "Do you think we should go?"

"Oh, for Pete's sake," he said. "You know how they exaggerate. The bad weather is still off the coast of Florida. It'll be days before it hits Long Island if it makes it there at all."

Was that supposed to calm me? The east coast of the United States experiences about five hurricanes a year, which can mean disaster for boaters and people on land too.

"But what about the fog, you know I hate it."

"Oh, come on, it's Maine," Gert said. This fog will lift by noon and by then we'll be out of the harbor and into the ocean. With the brand new GPS we have nothing to worry about."

I sighed. This all sounded depressingly familiar

I had heard all this years ago on *Hasard*, and we had covered many miles of local sailing since then. I was getting smarter about this sailing thing. We had also been married longer and my eyes were definitely less starry. I knew both fog and the unpredictability of electronics. Gert's mantra has always been: "Don't worry."

I was worried.

I heard a groan. Maggie May was now awake and I swear she had been listening to this conversation. Dogs are smart, and Maggie was no exception. I had read that humans do not rely on instinct and emotions like animals do. Maggie's big brown eyes said it all, and her instinct sensed trouble.

I believe Maggie had been secretly monitoring this whole

sailing idea that past year from the safety of land. She would curl up at our feet looking from one of us to the other as we talked of cruising. We had taken a little sailboat to the Florida Keys one winter – Maggie's first live-aboard experience. It had worked as we anchored nightly or pulled up to a dock to take her for a walk so she could do her business. The kind of sailing Gert and I were now planning would involve days at sea and did not include night-time walks. Maggie would have to be trained to go forward on the deck to relieve herself. This is not easy to teach a dog, especially not an eight year old.

Maggie was also a very active golden retriever and had never missed a day without a walk or swim, neither of which would be possible aboard. Frisbees, too, were definitely out.

I had bought her a lifejacket, a cumbersome orange thing with straps and clips. "You'll make her such a sissy," Gert said. She looked uncomfortable in it but I figured if she fell overboard, or the boat sank, at least it would give her a chance.

The shake-down cruise was about to start. At least this time we had a radio and a GPS, and Jim's math and spatial abilities; he would be able to decipher the charts until I became more confident. I was well aware, however, that Jim would not be there to assist me once we took off on the big trip.

As I checked our lifejackets I remembered what a friend had said years ago – that he wouldn't wear a lifejacket as the sharks would look at his feet floating below the water and consider them appetizers. Great visual. But I had grown wiser since our last cruising adventure: the lifejackets were at the ready.

We had a schedule to keep as both Jim and I had to be back at work Monday morning.

RULE #1 Never go sailing on a schedule.

We slipped our lines and started to motor out of the harbor around eleven am. We were quickly engulfed in fog, which was normal at this time of year in the New England area. It always burned off around noon, or so said the local folklore

No-one spoke as we ghosted along, Jim checking the charts

and me, in my usual position, staring into the fog, looking out for other boats and the buoy that marked the entrance to the ocean.

Jim went below again to chart our course and Maggie May curled up on the cockpit floor at Gert's feet. The sun was coming out and we were all feeling good. Gert, his face shining, looked like an ad for the Nordic Times. His first wife had described him as "a man's man". I'm not quite sure what she meant by that but he was physically strong, and attractive to many women – and to men for that matter. He was quiet when I first met him and rather shy. In many ways he is a loner but he was now definitely in his element, sailing his beloved boat.

I went below to make lunch. We had skipped breakfast as the excitement of departure had led to a drinking splurge the previous night which hadn't helped our stomachs. Beans and rice seemed like the perfect quick meal. Some hot chilies and a dash of tabasco sauce and we were good to go.

It was Friday morning. Our plan was to make this a straight run, sailing through the night, arriving at Long Island sometime late Sunday. The wind had picked up a little and we were able to set sails and cut the motor. The waves were coming in big rollers but *Zivio's* motion felt gentle and comforting, with no pounding: such is the beauty of a sailboat.

Later the motion increased. I looked out to see waves bigger than I had ever seen before. We would dip into a trough, then rise to the crest. In a trough you could see nothing but water all around you – it's a bit scary the first time. I tuned into the weather channel around three in the afternoon. The storm was strengthening and making a northward turn towards us, but nothing to be concerned about. Yet. At around six we ate more beans and rice, washed down with shots of Aquavit and beer. We set a four-hour sailing rotation with two people in the cockpit at all times. I went below to sleep first.

I awoke to a bang and tasted blood. I was on the floor and my nose hurt. Sea water was splashing down the hatch and everything was getting wet. "What's going on?" I screamed, stood up quickly and heard a crunch, I had stepped on my glasses.

Jim and Gert were yelling as I emerged, clasping my bloody nose. Jim clutched the wheel while Gert tugged down sails. I stared at the giant rollers tossing the boat and understood what had happened. *Zivio* had been hit by a rogue wave which had thrown me out of the bunk and unlatched the door to the head which then slammed into my nose. I grabbed a bag of frozen peas from our ice chest.

Already we were experiencing some of the effects from the storm. Gert yelled at me to come up while Jim checked our position. Clutching the frozen peas to my nose, I did as commanded, stung by his tone of voice. I'm surprised I didn't say, "Aye aye, Captain!"

"Are you alright?" Gert asked at last, noticing the blood.

I nodded. "It's probably not broken," I proclaimed, dramatically.

When all the excitement had died down, Jim went below to rest. Maggie crawled into the bunk next to him and I kept watch for ships. Within minutes Jim reappeared, hand clutching his mouth, to vomit over the side. So much for my beans and rice.

Gert made the decision: we would anchor for the night. Jim and I didn't argue. Between bouts of puking, Jim charted a course to Cape Kennebunk, Maine.

By the time we reached Kennebunk, we had been out at sea for twenty-seven hours. We made it to a dock that night and I don't know who got off the boat faster, Jim, Maggie, or me. Dry land never felt better. Jim called his wife to assure her we were okay. She told him she had been worried sick as it appeared the storm was moving faster up the coast than expected. He told her not to worry, though he was not looking very confident himself.

And me? I was terrified.

The next morning we woke early. Crackers and tea were all Jim and I could manage, but Gert ate the usual, eggs, ham, and toast with a big cup of coffee, all washed down with a shot of the usual. "Toast anyone?" he asked, wiping crumbs from his chin.

We sailed and motored throughout the day in the rough and choppy Long Island Sound. Maggie had squeezed herself into a corner of a bunk, with her paws curled over her eyes and no intention of coming up.

We motored most of the day and arrived late at the Cape Cod Canal where we treated ourselves to a dinner at the local marina. After a restful night's sleep, we sailed all the next day until we reached Fishers Island in Connecticut where we anchored and rowed Maggie ashore.

It was Tuesday. We were already behind schedule and had at least another day before crossing the sound and getting to our home port, Mount Sinai on Long Island. The trip had taken us almost four days so far, and Maggie had not left her bunk except when we had anchored. She did not look happy.

At last, after another day of sailing, we finally maneuvered into our space at the marina in Mount Sinai and hung out the fenders. Once *Zivio* was safely secured we all jumped into Jim's truck which we had left at the dock before the trip and drove back to the barn. When I opened the door of the truck, Maggie took off as though her tail was on fire.

Zivio was safe and secure at her new home and so were we. We had done it!

~

We lived on the boat in Mount Sinai that winter, even putting a little Christmas tree on the forward deck and throwing a New Year's party. The dock was expensive so that spring we left and took a mooring in the harbor, which meant that we had to row to and from land every day. This was quite a novel way to get to work, especially on rainy days.

We stayed there until the fall that year, then sailed to a boatyard in Connecticut. *Zivio* needed a repaint and Gert was still replacing old engine parts with new. Again, all those years later, working on the boat had become our weekend entertainment. Some colorful characters lived on their boats in that boatyard. You have to be a bit eccentric to live on board through a New England winter. I guess that is how everyone viewed us too.

Boat people, especially those who choose to live on board, view life differently for sure. For us it was all about living simply – getting rid of the stuff accumulated over a lifetime. I believe our decision not to own a television was the best we ever made. We didn't have commercials telling us what we should wear and do and think. When one of my students told his parents I had no TV, they warned him I must be nuts – who could possible live without one? To this day, almost forty years later, we still don't own one, and I consider my life the better for that.

While *Zivio* spent the winter in the Connecticut boatyard, we lived in the barn and continued to work. Gert had constructed a wall between his garage area and our living quarters, laid down a plywood floor, and installed a couple of windows. With a toilet and sink, we now lived in comparative luxury.

Work on *Zivio* was completed in late spring and we brought her back to Mount Sinai for the summer with the plan to move her to North Carolina where we had property and from where we intended to start our cruise. We had bought twenty-one acres of land during our working years – land was cheap in Pamlico Sound back then. We kept an old trailer on it and hoped to build our retirement home someday.

This time, leaving Long Island, we checked the weather carefully via hand-held VHF radio and had a blissfully uneventful sail on the outside, in the Atlantic, coming in right before Cape May and continuing on the Intracoastal. We secured a spot in Vandemere, North Carolina, up a small creek and close to our trailer. Here our plan was to hang out for a few

weeks before heading further south. There is always something
to do on a boat so we wouldn't be bored.

Maggie May would not be coming on our cruising trip. Gert
and I had avoided talking about the inevitable. She was getting
older, hip problems were already evident and it wouldn't be fair
to subject her to possible rough conditions. The decision to leave
her was the hardest we would ever make. Maggie was our baby
and you don't just dump your child because it no longer fits your
lifestyle. But that is exactly what I felt we were doing. That trip
from Maine to Long Island, a year and half ago now, had been
another deciding factor. I started making provisions for her to
stay with my sister and brother-in-law.

Meanwhile a hurricane was approaching, so our trip to take
Maggie to her new home in Buffalo was on hold for a few days.
In spite of the danger of hurricanes at this time of year, this is
when most boats make the north-south trek to warmer climes,
carefully monitoring the weather.

Gert had no intention of leaving *Zivio* until the bad weather
passed. He felt she would be safe up the protected creek where
we were working on her, and planned to stay on board to adjust
the lines as the water rose and fell, thereby minimizing any
damage. I was to take Maggie and drive our station wagon to the
shelter at the local college. Remember there still were no cell
phones at this time, so I had no means of communication with
Gert.

Dogs were not allowed in the shelter so I spent the night in
the parking lot of the school with Maggie curled up close to me.
Our neighbor, Mortimer, was parked alongside with half the cat
population of the county leaping around in the cab of his pick-
up. Inside the school building, there was a party atmosphere. I
guessed these people were used to these events in southeastern
North Carolina. I could smell bags of deep-fat fried chicken and
I was more afraid of that food killing me then any wind.

I kept my portable radio on and listened to the progress of
the storm. In spite of the slamming winds and creaking trees and

lashing rain, I didn't feel scared. I was on dry land and Maggie was by my side. I knew that Gert, tough as he is, would be okay.

The winds had stopped howling by early the next morning. I decided to return to Gert but, due to high water and debris, police had cordoned off the road to the creek where *Zivio* was moored. I spent most of the day on a side street, trying to read a book and trying not to worry. Around five in the afternoon, the police let us through. As I approached I could see *Zivio*'s mast in the distance, tall and straight. She had come through unscathed. Gert stuck his head out of the companionway and grinned broadly. He had survived his first fully-fledged hurricane aboard his boat – no wonder he looked triumphant.

~

We were still on schedule to leave in November and continued to stock *Zivio* with food and our few personal belongings. We even invested in a device which purified seawater so we could drink it – an expense but one we would be forever happy with, especially in areas of the world where water cost four and five dollars a gallon. But this was not the happiest of times for me. The air was hot and sticky. I fell while painting the boom, and shingles broke out on my leg, so painful I had to make a tent to protect it from contact with the bedcovers.

But a worse pain was to come. It was time to make that one last trip north to deliver Maggie to my sister.

North Carolina weather is unpredictable this time of year. Experiencing its last flash of summer, the temperature had risen into the eighties. We packed our car in air as steamy as the jungles of Southeast Asia. Not that I had ever been there but my imagination was working overtime

As I walked back and forth to the car, poor Maggie shadowed me. Did she know what we were planning? My tears were already welling and we still had a fourteen hour drive ahead of us. In the car, I sat in the back seat to hold her for the ride.

Gert thought it would be a good idea to take the scenic route west across North Carolina and the skyline highway on the way back. The weather should be good, he said, but it wasn't and by the time we reached the highway, five hours later, the road had been closed due to ice conditions. Only in North Carolina.

We took an alternate route and by the time we hit Pennsylvania we were driving up and down mountains covered in ice and snow. We finally made it to my sister's home but as we pulled into her driveway there was little rejoicing. I had become thoroughly depressed.

Maggie's big mournful eyes never left me. We didn't stay long. I couldn't bear to prolong the agony of parting. The ride back to North Carolina was fourteen hours of misery. What a way to be embarking on a trip around the world.

9

THE INTRACOASTAL WATERWAY
VANDEMERE N.C. TO GEORGIA

2003 - 2004

"Untie the lines," Gert shouted. Everyone shouts on a boat – either the engines are too loud or a disaster is about to happen. It was late fall and we had left Vandemere, North Carolina. The trip down the Intracoastal felt like old hat now, we had done it so many times. The clouds hung heavy, low, and the color of mud. No high winds were predicted for today but I have come to mistrust weather reports. The Bahamians say, "If you want to know the weather just look up". They were always right.

I untied the lines and optimistically curled them on the deck in neat coils, just like at the boat shows. I chuckled to myself knowing they would not stay so proper for long. Tidiness is not one of my attributes – my idea of packing is stuffing everything into a Walmart bag – but I was finding out how important order was when living in a boat. Knowing where to find everything is crucial, especially in the dark or an emergency like rough weather.

Gert slowly reversed her engines and I went below for the

charts that would guide us south towards Beaufort, North
Carolina. We would follow the same route as seventeen years ago
with *Hasard*. The difference was, *Zivio* was our home.

I reviewed our situation in my mind. We had spent most of
our money getting her readied and with only my small pension
to live on we were about to spend five years sailing round the
world.

Around the world!

How casually those words tripped off my tongue. But all
those articles about sailing into far-off ports, tasting and
experiencing the cultures of exotic places, had inspired me.
Besides, after a sailing class, I convinced myself I was ready for
this. I just had no idea then how my life would change.

Sailing and living on *Zivio* would teach me lessons I'd never
imagined were there to be learned. Most were about me and how
I would act and react to the world. Traveling, I have always said,
is the best education.

"Guess we won't be sailing much today," I said to Gert, "with
that wind on the nose again."

Gert shrugged. "Nothing surprising this time of year."

Unfortunately, the wind stayed on the nose for the entire trip to
Florida. Thank God we now had a depth sounder and thank God
again it was working. In the Intracoastal Waterway, which extends
from New Jersey to the southern tip of Florida and beyond,
shoaling is frequent and you can easily run aground. Prevailing
southwest winds often clash with currents off the Atlantic, creating
unsettling conditions that can move the channel markers so you
have to be aware of your position at all times, checking and
rechecking your charts and the depth sounder. It's not like putting
your car in drive and heading straight down the thruway.

Making things even more interesting are the crab-pot floats
and fishnet stakes just beyond the markers. You don't want their
lines to become entangled in your propeller and cut your engine.
You don't want to have to drop an anchor and dive under the

boat to slash through the tangle. Besides, the owner of these pots will not be pleased with you. My learning curve had sharpened to a ninety-degree angle.

We motored all day and anchored at night. While traveling I was constantly on the alert, checking charts, watching out for other boats, reading the depth sounder, or taking turns at the wheel while somehow finding time to cook meals. I was learning so many things but by the end of the day was exhausted. This had one advantage – I slept like a log, something I would give my eye teeth for now at the age of seventy-two. This constant action required a major adjustment for me at this stage of my life. Growing up on a farm I was no stranger to hard work, but there you could sit down on a hay-bale occasionally and have a smoke.

I started to wonder what the next five years would be like. Would I always be encased in a yellow rubber jacket like an Oscar Meyer hotdog? Would my glasses be constantly encrusted with salt from the ocean spray?

Because this was December, the time of unpredictable weather, we preferred to push on. No chance to stop and explore. The weather was cold and rainy much of the time and I longed to feel some sun and a soft warm breeze. Florida seemed far away.

Christmas Day was approaching and we were nowhere close to a town. The weather continued to deteriorate forcing us to stop earlier than planned. We checked a chart but found no designated anchorage. We took our best shot in an area called Mosquito Canal in South Carolina. It looked as if it might be protected from the wind so we slowly inched our way in. Of course, you know what happened next – that unexpected shoaling occurred and yes, we were hard aground.

Tension was mounting.

"I thought you were reading the depth sounder?" Gert yelled.

"Oh sure," I yelled back. "Was that before or *after* I went forward to unleash the anchor?"

We were frighteningly close to the banks of the river and worried that *Zivio* would smash into the shoreline. My stomach knotted as I stared into the water, looking for hidden rocks. *Zivio* had a six-foot draft and this water must have been somewhere between five and six feet deep.

Gert had an idea. "Quick! Let's get the dinghy in the water. I'll throw out an anchor and we'll winch her off."

There was a problem with this idea. It was clear we would have to pull her in the direction of the opening to the little cove, which we could not do without the use of the second anchor.

Gert rowed our little dinghy against the wind and let out anchor line while I attached the other end to a winch. With two anchors out, Gert rowed back to *Zivio* and we took turns winching and pulling. Despite the cold we were both sweating. A boat approached. The driver in his enthusiasm, managed to smash his boat into our side.

"Hi," he shouted, as if nothing had happened. "I just live across the way…I was watching you though my binoculars and noticed you were in trouble. Want some help?"

I looked at Gert, who was still sitting in the dinghy, now soaking wet and physically spent from all this rowing and pulling lines. I tensed, waiting for some choice language from him but he just glanced at the gouge in *Zivio*'s side and muttered, "No thanks," through gritted teeth.

The man smiled and backed his boat away. I think he'd sensed the mood.

After a couple of hours we managed to winch *Zivio* off the sandbank, move a few yards to deeper water and set anchor in the opening of the little cove. Gert clambered back aboard, panting and drenched with sweat. He went straight down below, stripped naked, took two – or maybe more – shots of liquor and collapsed wordlessly into his down sleeping bag.

I volunteered to sit in the companionway and keep watch,

taking slugs of Aquavit straight from the bottle. It was Christmas Day, I was cold and wet and I missed my Maggie. I wondered if she missed me. I know dogs are supposed to live in the moment but somehow I felt she was thinking of me. I envisioned her big brown eyes and wished so hard that she were here so I could assure her I had made the right decision – this was not the place for her.

After a couple of hours, *Zivio* started to move, swinging back and forth and then finally turning around completely. Have we talked about tides yet? Well, the tide was coming in or going out I didn't know which, and for the next six hours *Zivio* spun in circles. I was on watch, drunk, and worrying about my husband who was probably dead of a heart attack in his sleeping bag.

I will not repeat the words I uttered during that watch but I am sure longshoremen are familiar with them.

Merry Christmas 2003.

Savannah, South Carolina is one of my favorite places. Oak trees covered with Spanish moss, or 'Frankenstein' grass as my cousin Bubba used to call it because it looks spooky, as if snakes and creepy crawlies would make their home in it.

The plan was to stay for a couple of days for a post Christmas celebration. My older sister had moved to Atlanta, Georgia, and I gave her a call. "Sure," she said. "I need a break from being a mother."

"Great!" I told her, "You can spend the night on *Zivio*,"

Pat had never seen our boat and had no interest in boating. Her silence said it all, she had asked no questions.

She arrived early in the afternoon.

"The place reminds me of Scarlett O'Hara," she said. "I've always loved Scarlett. All sweet on the outside, but killer-instinct inside." Pat fancied herself as the reincarnation of Scarlett.

As we walked around town, she wanted to pick up a couple

of bottles of wine. I forgot to tell you she drinks. As, according to AA standards, do I. The drinking started early. She was in her glory – Savannah, the boat dock, the holiday season. She *was* Scarlett O'Hara.

That afternoon we met a couple from another boat who had just completed a circumnavigation and we invited them over, eager to hear about their voyage. I thought my sister might enjoy hearing what other people were doing, and what our plans were. My family had no idea where this sailing adventure was taking me or what it was all about – we were farmers, remember?

As the woman told fascinating stories of places she and her husband had sailed to, I noticed my sister eyeing her with 'the look'. Everyone acquainted with my sister knew what that meant.

I knew what was coming. It hadn't taken long. "Well," she said. "*You* probably don't have children. I have five and I'm a single parent." From the tone of her voice, she might have been saying she had flown to the moon singlehanded.

Oops, we were in trouble. My sister was going for 'the nasty', the way she becomes after drinking one too many.

"Actually," the woman said sweetly, "I brought up five children too, but much of my work I did at home. As a lawyer, I only worked away when I had to appear in court."

Uh oh, this was not going to be pretty. I grabbed Pat's arm and said, "Can you give me a hand?" With that I dragged her down the companionway towards the aft cabin. This was the point where my sister usually falls asleep which, thank God, she did before she could deliver any more insults.

The next morning after a few cups of coffee it was business as usual and no-one discussed the night before. My sister drove back to Atlanta and we motored on our way to St. Mary's, Georgia.

In St. Catherines Sound we finally raised our sails. The winds were gentle, pushing with us and not against us for once. The sounds can be rough, don't get me wrong; but on this day they were a peaceful change from all the maneuvering in small rivers and creeks that we had just gone through. I was still dressed for winter and rain and snow but somehow, just knowing Florida was near made it all seem worthwhile.

～

Passing the Sapelo, St. Simons, and Jekyll Islands, I remembered the trip in *Hasard*, years before, in our younger, newly-wed years. Looking back, I realized that discovering those places had been one of our most enjoyable times. We had walked those islands and felt the romance.

The day before New Year's Eve we docked in St. Mary's, Georgia. There we explored the town and provisioned for the rest of the journey into Florida. We started mingling with other sailors and listening to their experiences. Most were from the east coast of the U.S. and Canada – a mixture of young adventurers with small boats and budgets, and retirees with large boats and budgets, all looking for a warmer place to live. And then there were the people who, like us, were planning a world cruise. We compared notes about our weather-related experiences and we were clearly not the only ones who'd had mishaps along the way. It helped somehow.

My idea of sailing was changing; I was starting to realize that one of the best aspects of boat-life were the people we were meeting. I came from a big family, I didn't enjoy being alone. Gert, on the other hand, was one of three siblings and the only boy.

There is a place in the Riverview Hotel in St.Mary's called Seagle's Saloon which had become famous among boat people for New Year's celebrations. A group of us decided to meet there, have dinner and toast the New Year. I listened as one of the Canadians complained: "Hey what's with your famous weather? Didn't you Americans promise us sunshine this far south?"

The man's wife smiled: "No dear, I believe *you* promised *me* sunshine. I was perfectly happy to fly to Florida and rent an apartment on the beach – I took this trip to make you happy… but I'm still thinking of catching that flight." This, someone told me, was the couple with the fifty-foot motor yacht and crew. People, I realized, had different ideas of boating.

Another couple, from the Great Lakes area in Wisconsin, had brought their seventy-pound labrador with them. "I'd never do this again with a dog," said the man. He complained about picking up the crap, about the barking at every noise, and the dog constantly where he shouldn't be when things got hairy. This made me feel better about leaving Maggie.

The year was drawing to a close and everyone was feeling merry. At midnight, we wished each other a safe journey ahead and vowed to meet up or down the line. My New Year wish was that I would be warm. I realize this doesn't sound very profound but it was what I wanted most at that moment.

Gert doesn't make wishes. He believes things only come true when you do them yourself.

Later, we staggered out of the bar, drunk and laughing. Then everyone stopped still and gaped; while we had been celebrating, snow had fallen. In southern Georgia, where the average temperature is sixty-five degrees at this time of year and rarely, if ever, does snow fall.

I took this as another omen.

10

FLORIDA TO PUERTO RICO

After leaving St. Mary's we sailed the Florida Intracoastal Waterway, which turned out to be one of the most boring parts of the eastern sea coast for me. The endless condos and vast over-the-top homes, the palm trees, swimming pools, and manicured yards, left me unimpressed.

Traveling was tedious. At forty-two feet, our mast was too tall to go under many of the bridges and most of the time we just floated around, hoping to not crash into other boats, waiting for another bridge tender to raise another damn bridge. Out of sheer frustration, we ended up motoring almost the entire way.

Yes, you are saying, we could have gone on the outside, but this was January when the weather is unpredictable. Still unable to swim and with that undiminished horror of drowning, I retained a healthy respect for large, open bodies of water.

Florida – the land of the Sunkist Oranges – disappointed me. You either like it or you don't, and I didn't. The east coast, with its flash resorts and hotels seemed somehow surreal. In New York I used to find it weird, this migration of people, all pasty white, leaving for Florida in the winter and coming back either burned red or yellowish-brown from the sun.

But the weather was warm by now and the seas looked calmer, and we were only going as far as Miami. We anchored in a spot called Sunset Lake. The usual big houses built too close to each other with the ubiquitous plastic flamingos on the front yard. All too fancy for my taste. I got the impression that people in this area enjoyed looking out at pretty boats, they just didn't want the inhabitants of these boats landing on their shores.

South Beach – does it get more glitzy? The main drag along the ocean is bordered by hotels, high-priced designer stores and restaurants where a person stands outside like a barker in a circus, pushing the billboard menu at you and yelling out the specials of the day. Tourists in gaudy colors stroll by, exposing more skin to view than most of their bodies warranted. Beside them, in our beat-up boat shoes and clearly out of fashion shorts and t-shirts, we looked like homeless people.

I was starting to believe I didn't fit in anywhere anymore. Not on land and perhaps, some days, not even on the boat, if truth were told.

Our next stop was Key West where life is one big party. Boats of all kinds were anchored in the harbor. Not just sailboats but big, fancy yachts and fishing boats, and towering cruise ships. We met sailors from all around the world – Europeans, the tanned people from South and Central America, and of course, the sun-starved Canadians. I have always enjoyed being around different cultures. It was one of the reasons I had chosen a college close to New York City.

But something had changed about Key West since the last time we were here with *Hasard*: the crowd was growing older. Where were the adventurous young people, setting out on life with little in their pocket? Not here. These were the retirees who had saved all their lives for this, their place in the sun.

Tacky as it may be, we enjoyed our time in Key West. What

made it special was not so much the place but the fact that we met up with our 'make-believe' son. I haven't told you yet about Michael. He had worked for Gert in New York after graduating from college when, much to his parents' dismay, he decided to work as a mechanic instead of using his college degree in communication. We had always said if we'd ever had a child, we'd have wanted him to be just like Michael. He was adventurous and kind and we adored him. I thanked his parents for putting up with him for his first eighteen years, but he was clearly meant to be ours now.

Michael was working in the Keys on some guy's boat, taking tourists for parasail rides.

"Do you want a go?" he asked.

I was hesitant. It looked scary. But then I saw an elderly woman stepping off the boat after her ride and laughing with joy. She was ninety-three years old, she told me, and visiting from Denmark. How could I not go after that? The three of us piled in.

The boat captain knew just how to give his customers a rush, stalling the boat so the sail dropped them frighteningly close to the clear blue water – dipping his passengers' toes into the shark-infested sea, then swooping them upwards to the sky, leaving their stomachs behind.

The thrill was not unlike how I felt about sailing. The difference was that I felt more secure in the sky, which is stupid as flying in the air, attached by a rope to a motorboat, is probably not all that safe. After landing unscathed, the three of us just laughed. Another experience. What more thrilling way could there have been to spend Valentine's Day?

We ended up at Michael's backyard, actually his tent in someone else's backyard, eating raw oysters and drinking the champagne we had bought out of paper cups.

The next day we all sailed out to the Dry Tortugas, seven small islands seventy-eight miles off the coast of Florida, about a day's sail away.

FORT JEFFERSON, DRY TORTUGAS

Michael had taken time off from his job to spend some more time with us and see these islands. They had taken their name from the Spanish word for turtles and the fact that early mariners had found no fresh water here. Michael was looking forward to snorkeling with Gert, he said, and exploring the coral reefs, which are the third largest in the world. Or at least, *were*. Now they have declined by as much as fifty percent due to global warming, over-fishing, and sea pollution.

Michael fitted comfortably into our lives and our cramped quarters, and nothing with him was complicated. We always laughed that once he got over his compulsory two days of seasickness, laying on the settee with his vomit-bucket, he was an ace sailor. Just as well as later he would move to California, get his captain's license and deliver boats for a living.

Gert and I left Key West Harbor early to tackle the day sail ahead of us. On our trips, we always threw a hook off the back of *Zivio* and almost always caught something for dinner. Heading west through the jetties today I turned around and noticed a pelican flapping in the water behind us. To my horror, I realized it was caught on our line

"Stop the boat," I screamed to Gert, as if we we're driving down the highway and could screech to a halt in an instant.

Luckily, we were motoring as we hadn't yet raised the sails. The problem was we were between the jetties with no room to maneuver. Meanwhile, in another boat close behind, a woman was screaming hysterically, "You're killing the pelican, you're killing the pelican!"

This wasn't helpful. I seethed and wanted to bring out my PETA (Protection for Animals Organization) t-shirt and wave it at her. Did she think I was trying to catch a pelican for dinner?

Gert's cool head prevailed once again. "Cut the motor, I'm throwing the rubber raft overboard," he said.

"Are you *crazy*?" I wailed. "That bird is *huge*." I wanted to add: *Shit. I'm steering this big boat between jetties by myself while my husband wrestles with a pelican!*

Gert threw the dinghy overboard, securing it to the back of the boat with a rope. He grabbed the fishing line while the pelican squawked and flapped its giant wings. I thought Gert was just going to cut through the line but no, he seized the bird by its neck and – to my amazement – pulled out the hook!

Meanwhile the fruitcake was still yelling to the world that we were 'destroying the wildlife'. She's lucky I didn't destroy her – couldn't she see Gert was doing his best?

He released the bird and it flew off gratefully. He pulled himself back on board and dragged the dinghy after him. His bare chest was crisscrossed with scratches from the bird's wings and feet. I was still shaking. My hero. I wanted to yell "Screw you lady!" but restrained myself.

⁓

The Dry Tortugas were a seventy-mile run away. They are actually seven islands west of Key West, abundant with nature, birds and fish. Michael had only the weekend free and we would sail him back to Key West on Monday. As soon as he arrived, he and Gert jumped in the water to snorkel. I watched from the safety of the boat; I had no intention of getting into this water as my fear of drowning was as strong as ever.

Michael had heard one of the best places to dive was a nearby sunken ship where the fish were reportedly abundant. We motored to the area and dropped anchor. People had told us to look for the giant jewfish that was supposed to be in that area. Well it was there alright; when Michael dove off the boat he

came face to face with it, and leapt back on board as if he had
sprouted wings. When he pulled off his mask his eyes were wide
with terror. The fish, he claimed, was twice as long as he was tall.
Jewfish are not supposed to hurt people but sometimes fish don't
read these claims.

That was the end of their snorkeling. Drinking and eating
was all Michael wanted to do for the rest of the day, all
we *could* do anyway as there are no bars or stores, nowhere even
to buy water. This area is a nature sanctuary and you have to be
totally self-sufficient. The only way to get here is by boat,
seaplane, or ferry.

There is, however, the famous Fort Jefferson, built
strategically at the entrance to the Gulf of Mexico. We sailed
there and spent the day touring the massive fort which had been
built in 1861, the largest brick construction in the Americas
according to the guide. Although unfinished, it served variously
as a prison during the Civil War and later a quarantine station
for victims of cholera and smallpox.

The weekend flew by too quickly. Other than the Coast
Guard warning us on the radio that we were getting a little too
close to Cuba, there was no excitement on the trip back to Key
West. We anchored in harbor and said our goodbyes to Michael
at a local restaurant. Who knows when we would meet again?

Remembering the last time, years ago, when we made the
crossing to the Bahamas, I was not looking forward to it at all.
On that occasion we had been out so long, friends had contacted
the Coast Guard, convinced we were lost at sea. Yes, *Zivio* was a
bigger boat, but I had by now learned that any size boat can
have trouble crossing the Gulf Stream. In Marathon Key we
began our final preparations for the crossing. We would need to
fill our fuel tanks and check the engine one last time and Gert
wanted to change the oil. I went through our cupboards to make

a final shopping list for food staples we might not find in the Islands, like special cereals and nuts and certain spices. There would be no Amazon deliveries – did we have enough toilet paper? Shampoo? I was trying to conserve and not use paper towels. I insisted on my Dunkin' Donuts coffee though. I knew I would run out eventually, but since it was my drug of choice, I bought as much as I could stuff in those cupboards.

The night before the crossing I sniffed the air – was that diesel fuel I could smell? Gert looked at me and sniffed too. "Fuck," he said.

He searched the engine compartment for leaks. (The engine on *Zivio* was midship – in a narrow hallway that connected the fore and aft cabins). I looked overboard, praying I would not see a river of diesel fuel leaking out of the hull. Finally, wiping his hands and smelling like a gas station, Gert emerged from the engine compartment and announced: "It's only a small leak."

"Great," I sighed. "Just the way I wanted to start this crossing."

But Gert remained maddeningly upbeat. These glitches never seemed to bother him, because he knew he could fix them, I suppose. "No big deal," he said. "We'll get it fixed when we get to the Bahamas."

"*Are you out of your mind?*" I screamed. "It's hard to get repairs done in the States, what makes you think we'll find someone in Jimmy Buffetland?" I stood, arms crossed. "No! I'm putting my foot down. I will *not* cross the Gulf Stream in a boat leaking diesel fuel."

Was this another omen, like the snow in St. Mary's? My stomach knotted, my shoulders ached. I envisioned twenty-four hours of hell, willing the boat not to explode halfway across the Gulf Stream. I saw myself afloat for days in shark-infested waters. Or passing out from inhaling diesel fumes and suffering permanent brain damage. I warned you I was a drama queen. I haven't even mentioned the fact that, since we still had no self-steering, I would be behind the wheel for half the trip.

"Okay, okay," Gert sighed. "We'll look for someone around Fort Lauderdale." So, we headed back north with our living quarters full of diesel fumes. My head was throbbing as we pulled into a marina. We found a place, just a fix-it-yourself yard, but that didn't worry Gert, the skilled mechanic. We had to first drain the tank we had filled to the brim for the crossing. The fumes were nauseating, and my headache worsened. When the tank was empty, Gert searched for a place to buy a portable soldering gun. Then he wire-brushed the area and soldered while I held my breath and awaited the explosion.

If everything had gone smoothly, if we hadn't had this fuel leak, I suppose I would be feeling differently. But as it was I was getting cold feet. Who was I kidding – was I really ready for this adventure? We hardly spoke during the three days it took to make the repairs. I had a decision to make; was I going on this trip or not? But how would I break the news to Gert? The trip was his life's dream and I was ready to kill it.

"I can't do it," I quietly told him one evening. There, I had said it!

Gert looked at me, threw up his hands and walked away. What had I expected? This was not an afternoon sail. We had talked about this world cruise for years and I had always known it would be rough. But I wasn't thirty-five anymore, I was fifty-five. Still physically strong but my life had changed so much since our trips with *Hasard*. I had become more settled in my ways.

We went to bed without talking. I doubt either of us slept.

I lay thinking. Here we were at the start of our five-year adventure, and we'd already arrived at the turning point. I started to question why I had agreed to the plan in the first place. Sometimes ideas take on a life of their own and build exponentially. I enjoyed the sojourn on *Hasard* but then I had been more starry-eyed. In reality much had changed, and not all in a positive way.

Working in a psychiatric emergency room was highly

stressful. It can be a depressing profession and the thought of going back to it until the age sixty-five years did not appeal to me. During those years, we hadn't found time to do much traveling – something always prevented it, like lack of time and money. And, of course, we'd had Maggie May. The thought of simplifying our lives had appealed to me. And then there was that commitment we had made to ourselves after the *Hasard* years, that we *would* do this again.

⌒

The next morning over breakfast, we sat forlornly looking at each other. "Well," Gert said. "I want to continue and it seems you don't. Where do we go from here?"

"A divorce?" I muttered.

This had always been a private joke between us – a post argument olive branch. "Because if we're *not* getting divorced, we need to figure out what to do."

Gert's face relaxed.

"I was thinking during the night," I said. "I like living on the boat, just not full time and definitely *not* in long stretches in open water. So why don't we find someone to crew with you?"

I envisaged how I could work on land, then fly to join him in places I wanted to explore, do some easy sailing. I still had a teaching license and could substitute teach which would give me the flexibility of time off. It would also pay my travel expenses.

"Guess you've got it all planned out," Gert said.

And so began our search for crew. Our brother-in-law John would be a good first choice. He was a couple of years older than us, a geologist, and financially able to leave his job. I knew my sister – she would support this plan. And I would live with her and be with my lovely Maggie May again. It looked like a win-win solution.

John left his job and joined us in Florida. I had decided to stay with them until we reached the Bahamas and continue what

I knew was easy sailing down the chain of islands. I wasn't excited about a repeat of the Gulf Stream crossing, but since there were now three of us I was less worried.

At the end of the chain, The Turks and Caicos, I flew back to New York, my sister, and Maggie May. Teaching interspersed with sailing trips, this was the new plan for the rest of the five-year journey.

⌁

John stayed on board for close to four months, but he and Gert had their disagreements. I wasn't surprised. I understood how difficult it is to live in such close quarters, all your little – which turn into big – idiosyncrasies emerge. What you can walk away from on land is not possible on a boat.

There is truth to the saying there is only room for one captain on a ship, much as I hadn't wanted to believe it in the beginning, but in moments of crisis, of which there are many on a boat, you really want someone in charge who knows what they are doing. That someone was clearly not me. I resented someone correcting me all the time and so, obviously, did John. At Puerto Rico they parted company.

11

PUERTO RICO TO GRENADA

I flew to Puerto Rico and said I would stay until we found crew.

In Florida we had met a French couple whose catamaran had been destroyed in a storm. They told us that if we ever needed crew they would like to join us as they wanted to reach Australia. We knew nothing about them other then they liked to party; admittedly not great criteria for picking a crew. Adrian, an artist, spoke fluent English but the little English Gigi spoke seemed to deteriorate the longer we knew her. Or as her moods dictated.

Adrian had built their catamaran and cobbled it together again after it smashed into the rocks. Adrian was the one who impressed us, but Gigi came along with the package. Adrian was mild mannered and even tempered. The same could not be said for Gigi.

They were very excited when we contacted them, and eager to join *Zivio*. We agreed to meet up in Grenada where I would leave them to return to the States and continue with teaching. I would rejoin them all at a later date, somewhere in South America.

In Puerto Rico I met the cruisers that Gert and John had been partying with for the four months while I was away. The women were no doubt bursting to know why I had jumped ship. And a little resentful – they had all been sorry to see John leave and they knew nothing of me.

Most of these cruisers were island-hopping with no plans beyond wintering in the Leeward and Windward Islands and returning to the States in the summer months. Many of them had retired from well-paying jobs, so money was not an issue. They spent their lives entertaining visitors, shopping, and eating out in expensive restaurants. Their boats were made of fiberglass, easier to maintain than our wooden *Zivio* and were fitted out with equipment that Gert could only dream of.

The islands were part of what was called the Lesser Antilles of the Caribbean belonging at various times to the British, French or Spanish; the population was mixed race as the islands had been inhabited by Africans brought over as slaves in the middle sixteen hundreds to early eighteen hundreds, and intermarriage resulted in exotic-looking people with diverse exotic accents.

On the few occasions we dined out, we found the food exquisite. In the French Islands, like Martinique and Guadeloupe, the freshly caught fish is flavored with subtle spices. I can still taste the mouthwatering grouper, coated in fresh coconut, served to us in a modest shack at the roadside. The Islanders eat a lot of chicken, steamed and fried, that looks and smells delicious. I had never heard of many of these foods before, roasted breadfruit, fried jack-fish, and of course the staples, rice dishes with delicious shrimp and fish. Pure culinary heaven for someone like me who loves her food

Sailing was easy as we never lost sight of an island and it took only a few hours to sail from one to another. The beaches were pristine white and sandy, and divers needed no equipment in the clear blue water. The sun shone every day. The bars were filled with tourists on a two-week vacation. Getting tanned seemed to be their primary objective, that and buying jewelry and junk to show everyone back home where they'd been.

The Caribbean Islands have been described as the whores of the United States as their economy, sadly, has become so dependent on U.S. dollars. The Islanders want to sell and the tourists want to buy: it works for them both. But I would have preferred to see the locals involved in producing their own goods to sell instead of relying on so many imports. Rum appeared to be their main export. It was cheap, and everyone we met was buying gift boxes to take home. The boaters too, stocked up for the next long haul.

We were still set on our five-year plan, the world cruise but with adjustments, namely my coming and going, at least as long as our budget could handle it. My work in New York would cover my airfares, my pension would cover all other expenses. Unless we had a catastrophe. And one thing I have learned about sailing is that catastrophes are usually right around the corner.

The last island in the Antilles chain is Grenada, the island where cruisers prepare for longer offshore journeys – either south to Trinidad, east towards Africa and Europe, or west towards the Panama Canal and beyond, where we were heading. This was the place where you checked your equipment carefully because it was cheaper and faster to order vital spare parts from the States for delivery to Grenada, than to have them sent to South America and elsewhere.

We anchored in Mount Hartman Bay on the south side of the island along with a forest of other boats. Here we began to meet the international craft that had crossed the Atlantic. I felt quite impressed already. Weather-beaten sailors told stories of wicked North Atlantic weather, where sails ripped and electrical equipment broke down. Many crews left the boat the moment it docked, disillusioned that sailing had not been all fun and games as they had imagined. I, on the other hand, was quite clear that I wanted no long ocean crossing, Atlantic or Pacific.

We made friends with a French family. *Madame*, concerned about their safety and the unpredictable Atlantic weather, had stayed in France with the children and had joined her husband in the Virgin Islands. There were many such stories, where one of the significant-others had stayed behind, opting to join up later in their travels – or not at all. This made my own coming and going appear less unusual.

We got to know other cruisers. Everyone had a story. People chose the cruising lifestyle for various reasons; adventures-seeking, starting a new life, ending an old. Some were running from legal problems back in their respective countries.

On the water you make friends quickly, perhaps because you don't know if you'll see each other again.

We got to know George, a local with a smart head for business and a keen eye for making money. He went from boat to boat finding out what work people needed done then directing them to other Islanders who could carry out the work, usually a member of George's own family.

Born on the islands, he had done odd jobs all his life to support his family. His classic line: *A man's gotta do what a man's gotta do*, is one we still use today. George quickly became a buddy. We even attended his mother's funeral – very different than any other I had been to. Male relatives carried her coffin along the dirt roads singing, not just hymns but great reggae, as is the custom in the islands. After the burial, we were invited to the home of one of the relatives where we ate and drank rum for the rest of the day – quite the sendoff for George's Ma.

We had plenty of time to explore Grenada as we waited for the crew to arrive from France. The local Mardi Gras was in full swing so there was plenty of partying. We rowed to local beaches with their requisite bars and barbecue and dancing. We visited the famous waterfalls and walked the national park and, of course, took the tour of the local rum distillery. We spent our evenings with other boaters, all talking about their sailing plans

But things were about to take a turn for the worse. A storm was brewing in mid-Atlantic and the prediction was not comforting. The experts were hinting it could turn out to be a mother of a hurricane. And worse, it looked like it might pass close by or even hit Grenada.

"But I thought hurricanes never hit here," I said to Gert.

On the dock, cruisers were gathered, muttering darkly about the weather report. George, in his best British Island accent, tried to reassure everyone. "No worries. Hurricane not hit here in fifty years." He sounded confident and reassuring but it was clear everyone was scared. Yes, Grenada was supposed to be safe. Why else do so many cruisers drop their boat insurance when they get there? As the day progressed, faces grew longer. People stuffed clothes and valuables into duffel bags. All around, cruisers made preparations for the storm. Opinions differed – should you throw out a couple of anchors and stay in the harbor or tie yourself to the dock?

I looked at Gert with wide eyes, "So what are we going to do?" Gert did not miss the panic in my voice. We opted to anchor in the harbor.

I was starting to question some of these theories, no matter who was telling them. Our neighbor, a Scottish lady, looked doubtful.

"We're tying the boat to the dock. I feel safer tied to something stationary than bobbing out in the open water." She had not been keen on this sailing venture in the first place and things were getting heated.

Her husband, an accomplished sailor, tried to convince her. "A boat has a better chance of surviving damage anchored out than on a dock – especially a concrete dock like this one."

"And I have a better chance of walking on land then swimming in a hurricane!" she yelled back. "The boat goes on the dock," (Their boat hull was subsequently smashed against the dock – a total write-off. They returned to Scotland).

George, in his calm and steady voice was advising people to make their way up to the deserted hotel that overlooked the Harbor. We would be safe there. It was strongly built and the entryway had a stone arch. Architecturally there was nothing safer. Really?

So up the hill we climbed to the hotel. Bags of groceries and liquor made their way up too, and all ended up on an abandoned table we had found. What else do you do in a hurricane? Have a party and pray.

If you have never experienced a hurricane, consider yourself lucky. When hurricane Ivan started in force, we huddled under the hotel arch. From here we should have had a view over the harbor and the Caribbean but, once the wind picked up, we saw nothing but flying debris. The combination of wave action and wind sounded like an approaching locomotive. A low, long growl seemed to come from the bottom of the ocean. I clutched Gert in terror.

The front of the hurricane passed. We breathed again and awaited the eye, the lull before the wind resumes on the other side of the eye and comes back to hit us harder.

When the eye came, eerily still and quiet, Gert and others went down to the dock to survey the damage. The women sensibly voted to remain in the workmen's basement of the hotel, drinking anxiously to hide their fears.

But the eye was briefer than anyone expected. I guess it hadn't read the same information we had, that they are supposed to last a couple of hours. Once the men realized the lull of the eye had almost passed, they barricaded themselves into a concrete shower block in the marina. An Australian woman had taken refuge there. "I've never been in a shower with six guys before," she later joked.

At that point, Gert said, the roof blew off.

Down in the harbor, the water was churning so wildly I

could see nothing of the boats. As I stood under the safety of that arch, watching huge uprooted trees fly past horizontally, like something from *The Wizard of Oz*, I imagined this was what the apocalypse would look like.

The storm lasted just a matter of hours but wind speeds, it was reported, had reached a hundred and sixty-five miles an hour. When it subsided, I breathed again – I was alive! But what about poor *Zivio*? I was already thinking ahead: if she were destroyed, at least Gert and I had a place in New York to return to.

This was selfish of me as I look back. So many people on that island lost everything. Ivan eventually became a category five hurricane; the highest level on the scale.

It was early evening and still light when we mustered the courage to return to the dock area. Picking our way among fallen trees and debris, we walked in a daze to search for our boats. Almost all those on the dock had sustained damage. Those that had stayed in the harbor lay lopsided in the mango groves with their anchors ripped out. Some had even been blown out of the harbor entrance and lost.

My stomach was knotted with worry. Suddenly I stopped and stared. "Look!" I gasped, grabbing Gert's arm. "*Zivio* is still floating."

He looked where I was pointing. "Jesus, you're right!"

We borrowed a dinghy and rowed out. In the calm after the storm, the sun came out and it might have been any other beautiful island day. Except of course for floating debris everywhere and the smell of leaked fuel permeating the air. *Zivio* however, was upright, as proud as can be, just one of a handful of boats still afloat in the harbor.

"Unbelievable," I said, blinking hard.

We walked around, checking lines and fittings; only one of the three anchors had broken loose.

I guess that surveyor had been right: *Zivio* could sail around the world.

12

GRENADA AFTER IVAN

Yes, I do believe it was luck. We certainly were not the most accomplished cruisers; the boats of others with far more experience than us were totally destroyed. Many of the cruisers were distraught – those who had no back-up plan having sold everything to follow their dream of living cheaply on a boat for the rest of their lives. This life may sound idyllic when you're young, but you need a back-up plan.

We began the clean-up. The sails were intact – we had taken them down before the storm and packed them below decks. I was thankful we had removed all lines topside as they would have been ripped off. We pulled up the steel anchors; amazingly only one was damaged, bent and twisted by wave and wind action. Other than the wood damage to the combing, – the outside railing on the front of the boat hull – it looked as if everything else was intact.

We'd left our radio on in case anyone from the shore wanted to get in touch with us. Our Scottish friends, James and Isa, were on board their boat, sorting through debris and sloshing through water. We knew they would want to know how we fared; being one of a handful of boats still floating. I heard a crackle sound and an announcement came through the loudspeaker from one of the cruisers, an English, retired military man. He suggested all boaters meet on the dock at seventeen hundred hours – he couldn't just say "Five-ish". British retired military men always have an air about them that they knew something we common folk don't. We rowed back to shore to hear what he had to say.

"We need to band together," said the self-appointed leader "I've been through this before in the service. We must protect ourselves from the locals. They'll be out here soon, looting from our boats. Does everyone have a gun?"

"What is this maniac talking about?" I whispered to Gert.

He suggested we take shifts and report any suspicious activity. We should warn everyone by firing one shot; then everyone was supposed to get on their radios to signal where the looters were located, then jump in their dinghies.

"To do what?" I whispered to Gert, "Go out and shoot them?" This was getting too crazy, I told Gert and he agreed. We left saying we would watch for looters, but we had no gun, nor would we be jumping into a dinghy to do whatever they planned to do.

Back on board, Gert announced: "Since *Zivio* is still seaworthy, we need to get out of here now and start heading for Venezuela."

I folded my arms and stared at him.

"Venezuela *no!*" I shouted. "We need to get on an airplane and go straight back to New York." This was Grenada, where I was supposed to let Adrian and Gigi, the French crew, take over. "We've survived hurricane number two," I said, "and I'm not waiting around for number three."

Gert tried to calm me. "We need to think and reassess our plans. The airports are all shut down, you can't leave and the crew can't get here. This isn't about choice anymore," he said. "And we mustn't feel too sorry for ourselves. Think of the locals – they have no electricity and soon there won't be any food or water or fuel left. At least we have a home, at least we have stocks of food and water."

I sat down, wanting to cry. I was living a bad movie. These things didn't happen to kids who sailed "The Great Tire Tube." What had I gotten myself into?

In the end, we agreed to wait for a few days until the situation on the island had settled down. Unfortunately for us and poor Grenada, that didn't happen quickly. Soon we would run out of food, I realized. There was nothing to buy as most stores had been destroyed. Boats in the harbor were leaking fuel and my nostrils were filled with the smell of diesel and gas. There was no electricity on most of the island so at night, other than candles and light from the few generators around town, we functioned in darkness. Our stove was propane so we could cook, but many on the island were cooking over outdoor fires.

We walked the town and saw the destruction. Many of the Islanders' homes had been swept away, and there were few shelters. Families camped out on the beach. Aid ships began to arrive with food, clothing, and other supplies but, because of some sort of political hold-up, they were not allowed to unload. Schools had been destroyed so kids could not go to school. Roads were flooded and public transport non-existent.

Most of the foreign-born students of the Medical School had been evacuated before the storm but a skeleton crew maintained the emergency service. I volunteered at the local Red Cross but was advised, if I had a way of getting off the island, I should go. What few resources the island had should be used by its own people.

Gert, by a borrowed, single side band radio, managed to contact his crew. Since they hadn't been able to reach Grenada, they arranged to meet Gert later in Venezuela. We were broke but for about twenty dollars. The few automatic money machines in the town were not operating because of the lack of electricity. People couldn't even check out of the island as the customs building had been destroyed. If we left Grenada we would be doing so illegally, with no documentation to allow us entry into the next port.

And yes, there was looting.

One night we heard gunshots and decided to leave the next day. We said goodbye to our buddy, George, and our boating friends, vowing to meet up somewhere down the line. On September 26, 2004, five days after Ivan had hit and the day after my birthday, we set sail for Margarita Island, Venezuela.

I believe the storm had left me in shock. At that point, traveling on *Zivio* was looking less dangerous than staying on that island.

Sailing along the coast, we looked on in dismay. Poor, post Ivan Grenada looked like one huge garbage dump, with homes flattened, cars upturned, and stone buildings reduced to rubble. The fields were soaked and reminded me of giant mud pies. It looked as if a giant weed-whacker had run right over the entire island crushing all the beautiful trees and flowers.

I read that a month after the storm, more than eighty percent of the island was still without electricity. Farmlands were flooded, crops destroyed. As a large part of Grenada's economy was based on tourism and the boat industry, financially they were in ruin. It would take Grenada months to get back on its feet and the psychological effects of the storm could never be measured.

The wind had lessened as we re-entered the Caribbean. The waves were still quite high, but less violent and resuming their normal rhythms. As I think back, I don't remember being afraid on that journey. I didn't fear I would drown, like I usually did. After surviving a category five hurricane, an overnight sail was looking like that proverbial piece of cake.

Next stop, Venezuela.

13

GRENADA TO VENEZUELA

We sailed into Port Porlamar, on Margarita Island, about forty miles north off the coast of Venezuela. Friends Lilly and Jeff, leaving Grenada just before the hurricane, had arranged to meet us there. "*If* we survive Ivan." Quite the goodbye message. They knew something about hurricanes, having lost their boat in a storm some years earlier. In retrospect, we should have followed their example and left earlier, but we had decided to stick to our own decisions, right or wrong. After all, hurricanes didn't hit Grenada, did they?

It is interesting to me, as I sit writing, that Venezuela is front-page news again. The current president, Maduro, who heads a military dictatorship, is being challenged by Juan Guaidó, the head of Venezuela's National Assembly, as the country's legitimate president. The year we visited, 2004, Chávez was in power and people had it had enough. They were already suffering hardship, with short food supplies and unemployment, but when Chávez died in 2013 and Maduro took over, conditions deteriorated further.

We witnessed the corruption the minute we anchored off Margarita. Having left Grenada with no papers from the Grenadian Customs to prove it, we found ourselves in a vulnerable position. Without those papers, we were in legal limbo.

Lilly and Jeff had been on Margarita a few days and already learning how the system worked. We were to meet up with a man at a local bar and, for a sum, he would issue us papers which showed we had left from St. Martin, an island north of Grenada. That island just required you, if you came on a Sunday, to fill out your own papers and deposit them in their mailbox. Our new buddy had secured a supply of these papers and was selling them to sailors in need. We filled that bill so what choice did we have?

Margarita's white beaches beckoned, but there was no time to explore the island. After a couple of days, we left for the mainland to meet Adrian and Gigi off their flight from France. Venezuela would also be the jump off point for me, but not, hopefully, before we did some inland traveling. Exploring was what I was most looking forward to.

In mainland Venezuela we moored in the marina of Maremares instead of anchoring outside. We enquired about workers to repair the damage on *Zivio* and the marina suggested carpenters they could vouch for.

Down to our last few dollars, we urgently needed to arrange for funds to be wired from the United States. We asked around and soon learned that everything here functioned by someone knowing someone. The word on the dock was that a man named Carlos would change our money on the black market.

Two days later we received word from the marina office that Carlos was at the front gate, asking for me. Apparently, our friends on Margarita had given him my name. They had also told us to take a blank check with us.

"Why are they asking for me, not you?" I asked Gert.

"You look less like an international smuggler." He laughed.

I walked to the front gate of the marina, feeling like a character from a Robert Ludlum book of espionage. Carlos was waiting, dressed in black of course. He motioned for me to follow him to a waiting black Mercedes.

As we approached the car, the black-tinted front passenger window lowered and an older woman, her pearl necklace adorning a red silk blouse, invited me in perfect and polite English to get into the back seat. Carlos held the door open. I slid onto the plush leather seats with my new, post Ivan confidence. Carlos stood guard at the door.

"Where are you from?" the woman asked.

I told her.

"It is a shame you cannot see the real Venezuela," she said, with sadness in her voice. "These are hard times. We are rich in oil and yet our people can barely feed themselves. The government takes everything, corruption is everywhere and you must always watch that someone is not stealing from you." She smiled then, with perfect white teeth. "If you traveled into the interior you would see Venezuelans as they truly are, kind, open to foreigners and wanting to show you our beautiful country."

As she spoke, her red fingernails tapped a leather briefcase beside her on the seat. On her ring finger a huge diamond flashed. Poverty was no firsthand problem to her, I guessed. "I am told you need money. I must have a check from an American bank. Please sign it and write the amount you need."

"Shouldn't I make it out to someone?" I asked naively.

"There is no need."

I explained that we had come from Grenada where the ATM was out of action and I would need a thousand dollars.

She hadn't once taken off her sunglasses or ceased tapping the briefcase. "That will not be a problem," she said. Then she unlocked the briefcase revealing stacks and stacks of Venezuelan bolívars.

Oh, boy, I thought to myself, *this is really creepy.*

The woman proceeded to count out one thousand dollars in Venezuelan bolívars, twice the amount I would have been given in a bank. I handed her the check and she handed me the money which I stuffed into my purse.

She said a curt goodbye and rapped on her window. Carlos opened the door for me and, clutching my purse with the wads of bolívars, I was out of there in a New York minute.

Welcome to South America.

Months later, when I received my bank statement. The check, I noticed, had been cashed in Miami.

14

VENEZUELA

The plans to explore Venezuela were underway. I suspected *la Señora* who had changed my money was right – I was not getting a fair picture of the Venezuelans. The marina where we were staying was an enclave for the privileged, where boaters were moneyed and women flew in for cosmetic surgery. Venezuela is *the* place to get rid of those wrinkles cheaply.

Adrian and Gigi arrived and were happy to look after the boat while we went away. Lilly and Jeff, who had guests, wanted to join an organized tour of the interior, but Gert and I had never been 'tour people.' We preferred to use local transport, getting on and off when something caught our fancy. The other couples felt tours were safer than going it alone and I was to learn later they were right.

The cost of the tour, a two-day trip to the Orinoco River Basin area, was not prohibitive if you excluded the private plane ride to the Angel Falls. So, we agreed to join them. The deal was we would rent two jeeps, each one with a driver, and explore the interior with a local guide. I rode in a jeep with Lilly and Jeff and their dog Max. Gert and a couple from Spain rode in the jeep ahead of us.

We had not been driving more than four or five hours when

we noticed smoke ahead. "What's going on?" I asked Juan, our driver.

"Oh, more bullshit," he answered, tossing his cigar out the window. The driver in the jeep ahead was waving for us to slow down. "No big deal," Juan said. "People protest about everything down here."

I looked at the others. "Is he making this up?" A demonstration was not supposed to be part of the tour. Lilly clutched her little Max closer.

"This town, it is not happy with Chávez's choice of mayor," Juan added.

I craned my neck as we drew closer. Smoke, dense and black, billowed from burning tires that had been laid across the road to block traffic. People were shouting and waving flags and lit torches. Juan jumped out of the jeep and strolled towards the other driver, apparently unperturbed. Meanwhile the demonstrators were shouting louder. I don't understand much Spanish but I recognize the word *muerte* when I hear it. I just didn't know whose death they were demanding.

I was getting scared. Juan returned. "Don't worry, *caballeros,*" he told us. "This is nothing. Business as usual in Venezuela. We go back, take another route." I wouldn't have cared at that point if he had turned around and gunned it back to the marina. He could keep our money.

He slammed the jeep into gear, stepped the gas pedal to the floor and followed the other jeep across a field of patchy grass. Grazing sheep and cattle took fright and scattered, kicking up choking dirt and dust.

"I can't believe this," I gasped. Meanwhile little Max's eyes were bulging out of his head.

We ground across this field for probably ten miles or so, leaving a trail of dust behind us, and then reconnected with the main highway.

Juan was making futile attempts at being a tour guide, pointing out the beautiful landscape and vegetation, none of which I took in. The tour had promised a leisurely drive into the Orinoco Delta region, no more than a six-hour drive, with a night at a resort hotel for dinner and entertainment. It had sounded lovely, short and sweet. Now I wouldn't be surprised if we spent the night in a jail.

We rounded a bend into an ambush. A group of young boys waved us to stop. They were about the age of my eighth-grade art class in New York, only these kids were wearing tattered green camouflage outfits and carrying assault rifles. And, unlike my kids at school, these looked *mean*.

The drivers jumped out. "Stay in the jeep," Juan ordered, lighting up another cigar.

We stayed. Max was the only one who didn't look worried. Lilly began sobbing.

"We're American citizens," Jeff told her. "Nothing's going to happen."

I glared at him. "What guidebook did you read *that* in?"

In the front jeep, Gert – with his usual calm – turned around and silently mouthed: "Don't worry!"

This was a dictatorship in political turmoil, angry people were burning tires in the street, and now I was facing teenagers with assault rifles and was not supposed to *worry*?

The leader of the gang ordered the drivers to gather up our passports and follow him. We were to remain in the jeeps. We reluctantly handed them over – *would we ever see them again*?

Gert's driver quickly returned with the three European passports and said they were free to go. We would meet up them further down the road.

"Wait," I yelled, but they had gone. *Would I ever see my husband again*?

Juan returned empty handed, "Look," he said, "these kids just want money. How much do you have?"

Another confirmation of how the Venezuelan system works. We handed over our money, about six hundred U.S. dollars, and within minutes we had caught up with the others. We found out later that the boys had demanded money only from us, the Americans, and not from the couple from Spain nor Gert with his Danish passport. Did that tell us something?

That night we stayed in a small resort in the middle of the jungle. I wish I could remember the name of the town. We entered through locked gates, which was comforting after what we had just been through. The hotel was about two stories high and quite upscale after all the shack-like homes we had seen on the trip here. Our room contained a bed, a lamp, a sink, and even a toilet. Showers, however, were located down the hallway.

At the bar later that evening we met up and recounted the day's events. I looked around at the other people in the restaurant – all nicely dressed but wearing way too much jewelry for my taste. Obviously these people hadn't taken the same budget detour we had or those little boys would have relieved them of it.

After a dinner of delicious fish we were entertained by local musicians. Drinking rum, dancing and singing, what better way could there be to forget the events of the day?

Then next morning, after a breakfast of eggs and fried fish, we left early for the Guácharo caves, famous for the oilbirds. These strange birds hang upside down inside these caves as, for some reason, their feet have been rendered useless; they have lost their ability to stand and land.

The rocky floors are wet and sticky with bat droppings. The only sound is water dripping from the ceiling, hanging rock formations, 'stalactites' if I remember correctly from earth-science lessons at school. The birds, we were told, are nocturnal feeders and as soon as night falls, they fly out of the cave by the thousands. They are said to have an advanced echo-location system like bats, which prevents them from flying into the walls of the cave, or each other, or people. I felt I was in an Alfred Hitchcock movie.

There were bats too, but we had other plans for the day: to paddle up the Orinoco River in canoes. Fishing for piranha was also part of the tour. Not that I was keen to eat one but I *was* anxious to see the Warao Amerindians, the canoe people who lived in the jungle.

In the Orinoco Delta, the people live along the river edge. Their homes are built on elevated platforms nestled in the jungle. They were still living as hunter-gatherers although, with the popularity of eco-tourism, they now make wood carvings of local wildlife to sell to tourists. Their thatched roof homes are completely open, with no walls at all. They sleep on hammocks hanging from the roof. In the center of their living space, the kitchen area presumably, is a fire with a constantly boiling pot.

I tried not to stare; these were their homes, not some museum. I didn't take pictures either as they might have considered that rude. These people lived frugally, but they did have generators – and a box which gave off a blue glow. You've guessed it, a television! The beginning of the end for these people in my view.

The Orinoco is the fourth largest river in the world, said our guide, and the delta covers most of northeast Venezuela. The area is an important nesting area for many bird species – parrots, macaws, egrets, falcons, hawks, and many more. It is also home to probably every deadly snake – boas, anacondas, and coral snakes, not to mention crocodiles, jaguars, and giant sea otters – you name it. And now I was glad we had taken the tour as, call me a sissy, I don't believe I would want to canoe this area alone.

Yes, an amazing area. The money changer had been right – Venezuela's interior *is* beautiful. She also said the locals were warm and friendly but in truth I could not verify this as, so far, we had only encountered angry teenagers and protestors burning tires.

The carpenters were at work when we returned. repairing the

damaged combing. Gigi and Adrian had settled in, ready to take care of *Zivio* while we were in the U.S. Gert had a few money-making jobs planned, and the single side band radio was ready to pick up. This valuable piece of equipment would be his means of communication when he sailed far from land.

15

LAND BOUND

Gert and I have a strong relationship. Driving him back to Kennedy airport after the trip back home, knowing we wouldn't see each other for a couple of months, I fought to stay brave. Again, we were separating but it had been my decision so I couldn't complain. No tears fell but as we hugged at the airport we looked at each other knowing we wouldn't keep this up very long. We had talked of our next meeting in Panama, but there, while we waited for his flight to be called, the previously agreed on three months shortened to two.

On the eight-hour drive to Buffalo, I had a lot to think about. We questioned how long we could keep this up financially. I knew the further away Gert sailed, the more expensive the flights to join him would become. I battled with my feelings and reality and realized, to my surprise, I wanted to be on this trip with Gert.

I rented an apartment in Lancaster on the outskirts of Buffalo. It was cheap and they allowed dogs. That was the best part of my decision to remain on land – Maggie and I would be together. Lancaster is an old, heavily Polish community and it felt like living in Eastern Europe as people spoke little or no English. All the signs in the stores were in Polish and, as I am half Polish myself (my maiden name is Wasik), I found it comforting to hear the language spoken in the bakery and the butchers. It reminded of my time growing up near my Polish grandparents' farm.

Across the street from my apartment was the requisite Catholic church and a lovely back yard where my Maggie May and I took our morning walk. (I always picked up the poo, I know about sin).

Below my apartment, the owner of the beauty salon sat at a fold-up table looking out her window most of the day. She had fiery hair and a blotchy red complexion, both coming from of a bottle from what I could tell. She always had a cigarette hanging out of her mouth and her low cut Lycra top displayed very large bosoms. Her clients always ended up with the same hairstyle as her own but in various shades of yellow or red; no-one walked out with their original color.

It was bitterly cold that winter and I spent ages in the morning defrosting my car to drive to my teaching jobs. I would drop Maggie off at my sister's for the day. In the evening, Maggie and I would go for another walk behind some nearby industrial buildings. I would unleash her and let her run; the area was the end of the line for the train, deserted and lonely. I probably should not have been walking there at night as this was not the safest section of Buffalo. I was no doubt feeling sorry for myself and for Maggie; here we were, suffering cold and loneliness, while Gert was enjoying the sun and sea, sailing in the Caribbean on his way to Colombia.

I was torn between wanting to be with Gert and not wanting to leave Maggie again. Adrian and Gigi were on board so Gert would have help to cross the Pacific. But I decided, after the Pacific crossing, I would stay on board. Adrian and Gigi would have to crew for another boat in their goal to reach Australia.

Maggie May was thirteen years old and would never sail with us again. Leaving her behind had been torture. She was old for a golden retriever and having difficulty dragging her back legs. She was starting to fall when we took our walks and, as I never wanted her to be in pain, I spoke to my sister about end-of-life arrangements.

Crazy, but it was easier to leave my aging parents than Maggie.

There was a lot to think about in that couple of months on my own. It didn't help that the winter of 2004 was one of the coldest ever in Buffalo.

I never wanted to feel cold again.

16

SAN BLAS, PANAMA

January, 2005

Two months had passed since I had last seen Gert. We are both fiercely independent, not at all a clingy couple – we had decided before tying the knot, that if our marriage didn't work out we would split amicably. But we had spent Christmas separately for the first time, he in Colombia and me in Buffalo, and agreed on the phone that we'd never do that again. Two months apart was enough.

The plan was that I should rejoin Gert and the crew in the San Blas Islands off Panama. Hearing the stories of how hard the trip had been, I was so glad I hadn't been on board from the ABC Islands – Aruba, Bonaire and Curaçao to Colombia. Many boats had been damaged and a few even lost in high winds and rough seas. Gert told me about a sailor he'd met whose boat had almost been destroyed on that stretch. He had given him a copy of the Bible that someone had given us at a farewell party, and he hoped I wouldn't mind. Of course, I didn't. Neither of us are religious but we agreed that anyone who has been out to sea in rough weather had better believe in something bigger than themselves. We did.

Gert had found a boatyard off the coast of Honduras in the Bay Islands which could pull *Zivio* out of the water to check her for damage and repair the rips in her sails.

While I was still in the States, Adrian, had learnt that his mother in France had terminal cancer. He and Gigi decided to go back but wanted to rejoin us a couple of months later. I felt so sorry for them but their departure actually solved a problem as I would have found it difficult to live with another couple in such close quarters.

My flight from New York arrived late into Panama City where I was informed that the only flight to the San Blas Islands left early in the morning. These planes were all small four and six seaters. There was nothing I could do so I hailed a cab and asked the driver to take me to the nearest hotel. It was a rundown quasi bar. The driver told me to wait; he would run in and see if a room was available. There was and he insisted on walking me to the room. I protested but he assured me I didn't want to wander into this hotel alone at night. He was right. The hotel clearly offered more than beans and rice. He told me to go straight to my room and lock the door and not open it for anyone. Believe me, I didn't have to be told twice. There was no lock on the door so I jammed a chair under the handle. Music was blaring and loud voices penetrated the thin walls. It was going to be a long night. I didn't undress, I just sat on the edge of the bed and watched the clock. As soon as the first morning light shone through the shutters, I grabbed my backpack and walked the dusty road to the airport to catch a little six-seater plane to the island, and Gert.

It felt good to be back on *Zivio* but I sensed tension between Gert and the crew.

Panama is one of those places where I could see myself living. It has the solitude that appeals to me, with white pristine beaches and cool mountain areas, and a cosmopolitan city if I needed my New York City fix. The weather can be hot and muggy but I don't mind that as long as I'm not painting or sanding a boat. We spent our time motoring *Zivio* up and down little rivers and creeks, taking in the lushness of the country.

On the coast again we anchored in Bocas Del Toro, a mecca for young surfers from around the world. It was there for the first time that we raised the American flag off the back of the boat as *Zivio* was registered in the U.S. Prior to that we had always flown the Danish flag but, after a reminder from a Scottish friend that you're supposed to fly the flag of the country where your boat is registered, we decided to comply.

That afternoon, while were in the cockpit enjoying drinks, a tour boat passed by and passengers started shouting, "Yankee go home". We waited until the boat was out of view and quickly lowered the flag.

What a shame, I thought. I was not out here to engage in politics, but I quickly found out how naive this was of me. The rest of the world talks more about politics than Americans – well, until 2019, the time of writing that is. Americans tend to be isolationist in many ways and our knowledge of history – mine included – is narrow, which can be quite embarrassing. I was fast getting the education I'd never had in school.

We explored the islands off the eastern coast of Panama. In one little bay where we moored, a couple of small boys rowed out to join us on *Zivio*. They had come from a local school we had visited earlier in the day. While I made popcorn, which they had never seen, they drew pictures of the local fish and gave them to us as presents. It was a beautiful moment and I hope we left them with a kinder impression of the U.S. than those surfers had.

17

INLAND TRAVEL

We returned to Bocas Del Toro to the news than Adrian and Gigi would be staying in France longer than expected. After his mother's death, Adrian had a lot of legal loose ends to wrap up. We told them not to worry. This was our chance to go traveling. We left *Zivio* anchored in Bocas Del Toro. We had become friendly with the owners of a nearby restaurant who promised to keep an eye on her.

The plan was to head north to Tikal, the ancient Mayan ruins in Guatemala, using canoes, buses, and our feet. Traveling on land with Gert has always been fun, perhaps because I am less dependent on him than when I am on the boat, and therefore on a more equal footing. Travel has always been our bond and we were looking forward to it. Gert would later say that to drive around the world, if that were possible, would be his preference: sailing was simply a cheap alternative.

Leaving Bocas we walked across an old elevated railroad bridge that crossed the Rio Sixaola. We cleared customs and entered Costa Rica and from there made our way, by a small boat, through banana plantations owned by an American firm, Chiquita. Then we caught a bus for an eight-hour ride to Los

Chiles, Costa Rica, near the Nicaraguan border. Costa Rica is flanked by the Caribbean and the Pacific, with lowlands close to its shores and the Sierra Madre Mountains in the center. Viewed from the windows of our bus, Costa Rica appeared to be better off than other Central American countries we were to visit, possibly one of the reasons Americans were flocking to buy land there. The drug trade had not infiltrated this area as heavily as it had further north, we were to learn.

At one of the rest stops I picked up an English newspaper; which I always do no matter where I am, and reading the classified ads I came across one for a bulletproof Mercedes for sale. Was this an indication of what to expect on this trip?

On the bus we conversed with a local college student. He told us the quickest and cheapest way into Nicaragua was from Los Chiles by the Frio River on one of the small local boats. It would also be the most scenic way to travel as the river banks ring with all kinds of birdsong and tiny howler monkeys jump and screech in the trees. Oh, and alligators too, he warned us.

It was late when we arrived in Los Chiles. As the last boat had already left we realized we would have to spend the night there. Rooms cost fifteen dollars a night. Okay, so what if the communal bathroom was down the hall? I was just happy there was one. After life on a sailboat, a bathroom down the hall felt like a luxury.

The next morning, we walked to the dock where our transportation awaited, a traditional long-tailed canoe. In the canoe, about ten unhappy men sat in handcuffs and foot shackles, subdued by armed guards.

Bulletproof Mercedes? *Hmmm.*

We would learn these prisoners were Nicaraguans who had crossed the border illegally and were being returned after a night in jail. A normal occurrence, it seemed. Politically, Nicaragua was in turmoil. It also had the dubious honor of topping the poorest-countries-in-the-world list for years. Noriega had been ousted by the time we were there but everyone still spoke of him, some affectionately. The local people were just as poor as they had always been, with a lousy educational system, few jobs, and a huge homeless problem. As always, it seems the only ones who profit from these regime changes are the guys on top.

After the boat ride – with no sighting of alligators – we continued on a bumpy bus ride. In the evening, the bus pulled into a hostel in San Carlos where we were to spend the night. I'd thought we would sleep on the bus but, because of the political situation, traveling at night was not considered safe.

Our room had a shower. Fancy, I thought, until I pulled back the shower-curtain to reveal a fifty-gallon metal drum filled with water, and a pitcher – the same water for every guest who rented this room of course. I had no idea how often it was emptied but I was definitely not taking a bath that night.

In the evening, we walked to the harbor and ate at a waterside restaurant where the beer flowed, and listened to music. While I was gazing out over the water, I realized the sky was turning black. A huge cloud was approaching. Gert and I watched, puzzled, as people began to vacate their tables and walk, then run, up the hill towards the town. Should we be doing the same? We did. The cloud, we had suddenly realized, was a swarm of buzzing mosquitos that surrounded and attacked us we ran back to our hotel. As we shut ourselves into our room they were still with us, seeming to cling to our clothing.

"Don't turn on the light!" I shouted to Gert.

Swatting frantically, we dove into bed and pulled up the sheets, but the little beasts still managed to creep under the bedclothes all night. The following morning, our skin looked like a connect-the-dots game board.

The next morning, we drove on to Managua, another six or seven-hour bus ride. The city had been almost totally destroyed by volcanoes in the 1990s but here we were, in 2005, and reconstruction was only just starting. Managua was an extreme mix of poverty and wealth. On the dirt-covered hills, deep in mud because of the torrential rains, people were living in houses made of cardboard boxes and tin sheeting. Yet further into the city you could catch glimpses of huge expensive homes surrounded by metal gates and high concrete walls.

On the outskirts of town our bus pulled up outside our hostel. Heavy metal gates opened into a courtyard and clanged quickly behind us. We were warned not to go outside the gates at night and that the bus would leave promptly at six in the morning. I unpacked the sheets and towels we traveled with – one of the precautions I take on our travels, hoping in this way to escape some deadly disease. At the snack bar we bought plates of beans and rice – not exactly a four-star restaurant but when you're hungry, it works.

The hotel we stayed in the following next night was hardly safer. We realized this when the hotel owner escorted us from the bus station carrying a metal pipe for protection. Not comforting. We didn't need to be told to not go out that night.

⌁

We were no longer traveling on tourist coaches but taking the 'chicken buses' the locals traveled on, colorfully painted but filthy inside. The seats were tiny as these had originally been school buses. But the tickets were cheap and I figured, if the buses were good enough for the locals they were good enough for us. Besides, scruffy and dusty, we looked pretty poor ourselves.

There is poverty in the U.S. but even our poorest looked well off compared to what I saw in Nicaragua. The buses were always crowded and if you didn't grab a seat you could end up sitting on a bag of beans or flour. Boxes of cabbages, stalks of plantains, bags of coffee and rice blocked the aisles. There was usually a dog in tow – which I never minded – or a couple of chickens in a cage sitting nearby.

People tried to converse with us in their broken English. They were curious about our boat travels, and I replied in my faltering Spanish. One of the passengers invited me to taste her *chimichurri* a delicious sauce called made of garlic, oil, and herbs that they pour over their meats, especially the chicken that was the staple in Central America, skinny and diseased-looking creatures, but it's okay when you're hungry. We ate so much I vowed that, when we got back to the U.S., I would never touch chicken again.

This rough style of travel may not suit some, but for me it made the adventure more exciting. You can read all you want about a country, but traveling and talking to the local people, seeing where they live, what they eat, and how they react to you is the only way we can ever truly understand – and hopefully accept – each other.

It seemed that if we had any trouble at all in Central America it was not with the average person, but always tied in with some political, military issue. Just before we left Nicaragua, our bus was stopped by Nicaraguan paramilitary toting machine guns. We were ordered to get out of the bus, taking our passports with us, women on one side and men on the other. Everyone looked scared but there was nothing for it but to do as ordered. They walked down the line checking our passports. After plucking a couple of people from the line, they ordered us to get back on the bus. I was sweating and it wasn't just from the heat.

18

COLÓN AND THE PANAMA CANAL

Anchored in the harbor in Colón, we waited for the crew to return, after which I would be returning to the States. As long as I had work in New York I could afford to fly in and out, at least for now. So far, this back-and-forth plan was working out. I could enjoy the traveling. I could avoid spending time in close quarters with strangers – three days is enough I always say. And, not least, I could dodge the long passages at sea.

I was not going to cross that ocean despite Gert's claim that Pacific means peaceful. I remembered a remark one of the women in Grenada made to that assertion. "Yeah, but someone has forgotten to relay the message to the Pacific." She knew what she was talking about from experience. "Pure hell," was her verdict.

I knew that once Gert and the crew crossed the Pacific I would have to make a serious decision: to stay on the boat or stay in New York. In the latter case, the trip around the world would be over for me.

We used the waiting time to sand and paint; the constant and backbreaking effort of *Zivio's* upkeep. As much as I hated the look of fiberglass boats, I knew what our next boat would be made of. (Yes, there would be a next one)!

We rowed ashore. Colón has the reputation of being especially dangerous. It is Noriega's home away from home. Word had it he was liked by the locals, or more likely, feared. Like all harbor towns Colón has a wide variety of characters and nationalities. From the marina (surrounded by razor wire) you could walk into the part of town where open-air fish, vegetable, and fruit markets vied for space with barber shops and cheap clothing stores. We strolled along narrow sidewalks, where tiny stores crowded side by side were stocked with everything from frying pans to women's underpants. All cheaply made – you were not going to see Prada here.

Gert got one of his many international haircuts. The barber's shop was a chair on the sidewalk, and a very large woman wearing a colorful low cut blouse motioned for Gert to sit. She then reached into a box filled with razors and brushes. I didn't see any running water but she would occasionally dip her comb into a bucket while cutting Gert's hair. Considering the circumstances the cut wasn't too bad.

When one of the boaters heard about the experience he said it was lucky Gert hadn't got his throat cut instead of his hair.

As a reward for our efforts on boat maintenance, we took time off to bus to Panama City. It was the first big town we had visited since starting this trip. Everything you could need was there – movie houses, upscale grocery stores, fancy restaurants.

We wandered through the streets and markets but didn't stick around too long as city visiting is a great way to empty your pockets.

The wait in Colón was also a good opportunity to connect to the States. Paperwork follows you everywhere when you haven't totally cut all ties to land. There were still taxes to be paid on our property in North Carolina and we needed to contact our friend Jim to make sure there were no problems with the heating or water systems in the New York barn. Gert decided to call his sister, Liss, in the States. They have always been close but, due to all the traveling, he had not called her in months. I sat next to him as he talked and heard the worry in his voice.

Gert was not an outwardly emotional person; he accepted what life brought and didn't try to fight the inevitable. His mother was eighty-seven years old and had macular degeneration and two recent falls had resulted in a broken hip. She was in Denmark and being cared for by her daughter, Gunn, and wanted her three children to come home. She was refusing all medication, even though she knew she would die without it. I felt bad for Gert. He remembered his mother as she had always been, a healthy and vibrant woman.

We talked it over that evening. His dad had passed away when we were sailing on *Hasard* in the Bahamas but back then we could both afford to fly back to Denmark. Circumstances were very different now. We were anchored in Panama, a potentially dangerous part of the world. We'd already had one dinghy stolen which had not filled us with confidence. What should we do? We didn't know when the French would return. Tickets were not cheap from this side of the world and money was tight.

"Look," I said eventually. "I'll stay on *Zivio* while you fly home." I was feeling brave now, safely back on board the boat. "But we must move *Zivio* onto the dock," I added. "There's no way I'm sitting out here on anchor and rowing in each day."

Within a couple of days, Gert was on an airplane to Denmark and I was tied up to the dock in Colón.

ALONE.

⌒

As it happened, I was hardly ever alone. Little by little, word got out on the dock of a single woman aboard an old wooden sailboat from the U.S. I must have been the talk of the dock bar as a continuous flow of boaters, both female and male, dropped to see how I was doing. I even began to enjoy this time alone on *Zivio*. I felt my old independent self again. However, I will come clean; I did have someone to spend the night on board and keep me warm. A stray cat wandered in one day from I know not where. His fur was ginger and I named him Panama Red. I'm not usually a cat lover, but he was good company.

As people dropped by, I became the dock therapist as I listened to complaints from other boaters about their husbands, or wives, or crew. I realized we were all in the same boat, if you'll excuse the pun. Cruising isn't always fun and games. Living in close quarters is not easy.

I met a couple who were probably in their early eighties. Their boat was falling apart and covered in seaweed and yucky growth. I would walk to their boat with my morning coffee and listen to the amazing stories, the boat adventures they'd had when they were younger. They had lived in South America for most of their lives, in the area Gert and I wanted to explore next, so I was doubly enthralled.

I was later to learn that the man's son had come from Texas to find that his father could hardly move due to an advanced state of diabetes. He'd arranged to have his father airlifted to a hospital. I guess the son never cared for his dad's companion, as he left her behind in Colón. She had no children or family to speak of, so who knows where she ended up.

RULE #2. Never grow old and sick on a boat. As much as

Gert loves sailing and living on board, he always said you needed a land base to return to.

⌇

Sitting in the marina bar one night I met a charming French couple, Claude and Renée, who were on their way to Tahiti with their two daughters, Babette and Suzie. They needed crew to transit the Canal so I signed on. Why not? I was probably a little drunk at the time.

It takes four people to sail through the canal. As your boat is lifted from one level of water to the next you are constantly throwing lines to workers on both sides of the locks. There are four locks to pass and halfway through the canal you anchor for the night. I was feeling quite proud of myself – here was I, this farmer's daughter from Lockport, New York, crewing on a French vessel through the Panama Canal.

The daughters entertained me the night I spent on board. I heard their take on being teenagers on a boat. It was mostly all positive, but they were approaching the boyfriend stage and there weren't any teenage boys around. They were home schooled and I was impressed by their sophisticated view of their travels and people they had met. The family decided to settle in Tahiti as the parents wanted their children to have a broader view of the world than they would if they had stayed in France.

On the last night, Claude and Renée served a memorable French meal of canard confit – pressed duck in white wine, canned and brought from France. Normally I hate duck but this was probably the best meal I had eaten in months. I slept well that night; maybe the wonderful French wine had something to do with that.

Next day we made our tearful goodbyes; even after such a short time together we felt connected. We separated with promises to meet up again in Tahiti and I traveled back to Colón via bus.

Gert's mother had only days to live but insisted he use his return ticket and come back to *Zivio*. She had seen her son again and was content. So, three weeks later, Gert flew back, the crew returned, and the cat departed in a huff. Time for me to return to the U.S. to make money.

19

ECUADOR AND PERU

After a cold winter in Buffalo, I arrived in Ecuador in March to thaw out. When Gert met me at the airport we vowed never again to spend so long apart. These traveling adventures were much more fun together yet, it had to be said, we also needed space and that was something you didn't have on a boat. But we would work it out, we always did. We left the airport, grabbing a bus which would take us to the anchorage where *Zivio* was moored.

Adrian and Gigi were on board. Their expression showed they were less than excited to see me, and I suspect I wasn't giving off positive vibes myself. I saw them tanned and happy in Ecuador on MY boat, while I was pale and drawn from a winter of work in Buffalo. Jealousy reared its ugly head yet who could I blame for this but myself?

That evening we rowed to the nearby marina restaurant where everyone seemed to know everyone else and I was feeling good and sorry for myself. After dinner, we talked over the upcoming trip. One couple would remain on *Zivio*, we agreed, while the other would travel inland. As I badly needed a holiday, everyone agreed that Gert and I should go first.

I had brought back a map of South America and in the next

days we made plans – well as much as Gert and I ever made plans for anything. They usually involved turning up at the local bus station and heading somewhere. In this case Machu Picchu would be our destination, that much was certain. I felt my excitement mounting. We bought bus tickets, packed some food to save money and we were off.

Surely few people can enjoy bus travel as much as I do. It allows me time to absorb a country and get a sense of the changing landscapes – in this case the desert on the west coast of South America and later the mountains of the Andes. Looking out the window on the Pacific I was reminded that we would soon be making the crossing to the Galápagos Islands. An easy trip – nothing like the dreaded Pacific Ocean crossing that Gert and crew were shortly to embark on – but I felt somehow smug. By this time I had completed several offshore trips, for days at a time even. Still, at that moment, it did feel good to be on the dry land of South America.

As we followed the steep and tortuous roads of the Andes, I began to feel nauseous and light-headed. I couldn't understand what was happening and of course by now, you know me, I immediately concluded I had dengue fever. When I finally accepted the diagnosis of altitude sickness, my fellow bus buddies told me the only cure was chewing coca leaves or drinking a coca leaf infusion. That explained why so many of the locals were chewing – and spitting, which I found rather disgusting. A familiar sight was a Peruvian with a rag thrown over their shoulder which they would use to wipe their mouth after spitting. And they spit anywhere, including on the bus. I bought a supply of leaves from a street vendor and threw them in my backpack and in a very short time I was chewing right along with them. Good that chewing coca was legal in that part of the world.

In our hotel in Cusco I lay in bed sipping coca tea. It had a mildly sedating effect on me. Luckily, the nausea and dizziness subsided and I was ready the next day to take a train to Machu Picchu, one of the Seven Wonders of the World.

The journey takes four hours. As the train wound through valleys and mountains, lush and green and warm, Buffalo was far from my mind.

We bought our entrance tickets to Machu Picchu and tagged along behind a group of tourists who had paid for a guide. Discretely hanging back, we were still close enough to catch the history of this mysterious Inca city. It is difficult to understand how, in the fifteenth century, a place like this could be built with primitive tools, and yet we couldn't get good phone connection in areas outside New York City. I was hoping to feel some pull from the spirits that reportedly filled this city but I will be honest, Tikal in Guatemala had felt more magical. You'd have thought, with all those coca leaves I might have felt a little *something*.

After a day of walking around the ruins, we boarded a late afternoon train back to Cusco. It was so crowded that Gert and I sat in separate compartments. He spent the trip with some rowdy tourists while I ended up sitting next to an old, serious looking Peruvian man. He didn't speak the whole way but would occasionally poke me in the side and indicate something he thought I should be aware of. Finally, he pointed to the mountains and said "snow" and I was tempted to tell him about Buffalo. I later learned he was a shaman who had been leading a group of people through the area.

Gert wound his way back down the train to tell me we were nearing Cusco where we would be getting off. After he returned to his compartment, the shaman tugged my sleeve and told me not to get off there. Hey, he was a shaman. I listened. "Take the train to the very end, to the Sacred Valley," he intoned.

At Cusco, when Gert came back to join me, I calmly shook my head. "No, we're not getting off here." He looked at me as if I had two heads. I explained the shaman's solemn instructions and he shrugged. That is one of Gert's attributes – he is open for anything, so if the shaman had ordered it, who were we to argue?

When the train pulled into Cusco I started to doubt my decision when I realized that everyone, including the shaman, got off in Cusco.

Well, we did continue on that train until the end and it was definitely a lucky move.

In spite of the late hour we found a B&B not too far from the train station. Rain had just fallen and the streets were pure mud. I was starving and asked the hotel owner where we could find a bite to eat so late. He told us to follow the muddy path and knock on the green door. The owner was a friend and he was always open.

Other than the owner, we were the only people at the restaurant. To our surprise delicious warm bread appeared on our table and within minutes a delicious meal of fish and rice was brought out. While scraping our plates clean we listened to the fascinating stories of the cook, who had trained at a culinary school in New York. He told us of his Australian friend, our B&B owner, who had apparently come across and bought the place after cycling, yes, I said *cycling*, around the world. You meet a lot of interesting people off the beaten track.

But tomorrow was another day and we planned an early start. A scribbled check arrived, another pleasant surprise. This five – no, *ten-star* dinner, complete with wine, had cost twenty dollars. In New York, we reckoned, it would have been closer to two hundred dollars.

The next day we hired the local cabbie to drive us around the valley. This was not a tourist area and there was no public transportation so if you didn't have a bicycle or mule this was *it*. Unless you wanted to walk.

The land in the valley was hilly but richly fertile. I admired how the locals farmed with oxen and primitive tools. We walked around the archaeological area of Moray – several terraced circular depressions where Inca ruins had been discovered. They looked to me like Roman amphitheaters. I knew now why the shaman had directed us here. I can't explain why but the area felt somehow more spiritual to me, maybe because of the simplicity or the lack of busloads of tourists scrambling for stuff to buy.

Our main problem here was the mud; the hired taxi proved not to be entirely reliable and at one point we ended up pushing it out of the mud when it got stuck. I did feel I should have received a discount on that ride.

I took a photo of three Indian children walking down a dirt road with a puppy. They were staring at us as only children do, open and friendly. Somehow I saw myself, back on the farm. Perhaps people are not as different as we imagine.

⌒

It was time to start our trek north. I felt a need to visit a big city again and it looked like Lima would fill the bill. Lonely Planet in hand, we searched for a B&B. Affordable accommodation is often located in the seedy parts of towns and ours was no exception. We took off on foot for a rapid tour of the museums, hoping not to return late to the hotel as, once again, we had been warned about going out at night. The next morning, as we left the hotel and walked down one of the side streets, we were to find out why. On the sidewalk, a big piece of cardboard concealed what would turn out to be a dead body. Yes, a dead body. Blood ran from under the cardboard into the dirt. This was a heavy drug area and someone, it appeared, was not happy with their deal. The person had apparently been shot. My first homicide. Time to leave Lima.

⌒

Heading north we decided we could not miss a trip to the Amazon River. From a town called Iquitos, considered the

gateway to the tribal villages of the Amazon, we could probably
– according to a local – hitch a ride on a barge to take us up the
river.

But, at the local bus station we found out that no roads led
to Iquitos. The only way to reach it was by airplane. Magnificent
– we would see the jungles of Peru from the air! Planes departed
from Lima to Iquitos four to five times a day. The fare was quite
reasonable – around seventy-five U.S. dollars one way for the
two of us. The eight-seater plane looked pretty flimsy but it was
only a two-hour flight. And besides, I was too excited to be
nervous. Here I was, flying over the rainforest in Peru, my eyes
glued to the window. We flew fairly low which made for great
viewing of lush, green forest. Below us, we were told, lived
various Indian communities. I did wonder if there were
headhunters down there and what would happen if the plane
crashed.

❦

Arriving in Iquitos in northern Peru we went straight to the
docks to enquire about barges traveling west. Waterfronts have
always fascinated me. They are even more exciting if you are
planning a boat trip. We would be traveling in the same way the
people living along the Amazon did, at that time there was no
other access than by small boats or these barges. We asked
around and found a working barge with a Captain who was
willing to take us. The trip would take three or four days, the
captain said. We could then catch a bus in Quito, Ecuador
which would take us to the coast, and *Zivio*. The barge would
leave in three days.

I looked on the internet to see what they had to say about
Iquitos. It was a boom town, I read, inhabited by wealthy
businessmen from around the world who were raping the land
for rubber from the trees and for the lumber itself. The town was

likened to those of the Wild West of America and brothels were big business.

We wandered around a local market where everything was for sale. We bought hammocks for our upcoming barge trip, but passed on the snake that was also for sale. The area, we were to learn later, has the reputation of being extremely dangerous and mugging and theft are common occurrences. I am glad we didn't hear all this before going but I guess it explained some of the wary looks we were getting from the locals.

On the outskirts of Iquitos is the town called Belen where all the houses are built on stilts in the water. This was a place we had to see but first we needed a boat. A local told us to go to the market on the edge of town as everything could be had there. We located the market but finding someone to row us around was more difficult. We'd been warned not to speak with any of the children as the area was infamous for child kidnappings. Body parts for transplants were procured here for wealthy foreigners. Yes, body parts. It's disgusting what money can buy. Eventually, one of the shopkeepers introduced us to a young man named Juan. For five dollars he agreed to row us around Belen but first, he said, he had to row to his home to put on a clean shirt. I didn't ask. In his freshly pressed shirt Juan rowed us up and down the river all afternoon, proudly pointing out the highlights. People bathing, women washing dishes and scrubbing clothes, kids floating in tire tubes, teens playing basketball. Yes, basketball. It all took place in the water. I was sorry when the little tour was over but Juan grinned as he pocketed his five dollars, plus a generous tip.

The day for the barge departure finally arrived. As we carried our backpacks and newly bought hammocks to the dock, I felt breathless with excitement. I was about to cruise the Mighty Amazon.

The carnival atmosphere was heightened by the colored clothes of the Indians, the oranges and yellows and reds of the multi-layered skirts, and the variety of distinctive hats. The loading of, often reluctant, animals added to the excitement as we boarded, weaving our way through squawking chickens, oinking pigs, and belligerent mules to secure a spot on the upper deck. We staked out our little spot and hung our hammocks to the roof, never letting go of our backpacks as we had been warned that thieving was just as common on board as on shore. We were the only tourists on board but we probably looked as poor as the locals, and what did we have worth stealing anyway?

The three-story commercial barge was rusting and grimy but everything paintable had been given a hasty lick of paint, by hand I am sure, in a startling blue. I leaned over the railings to gaze down at the wharf from above. The smells from the animals, intensified in the humid heat, wafted up to us on the third floor. A pig squealed, indignant to be tethered by one foot. The grey of the sky could not dull the vibrancy of the colors of the people and the cargo waiting to be loaded. Surveying the scene, I felt I was looking at a movie set. I know that sounds weird, maybe because I've always lived in a fantasy world, but it's true. The scene was so dramatic I wouldn't have been surprised to see soldiers come charging by on horseback, with guns flashing like in some B-movie.

Down in the water, tons of timber floated haphazardly to be either milled or floated further down the river. Creepers were growing from some of the logs, they had been there so long. It saddened me to see the sheer quantity, knowing I was witnessing the destruction of the Amazon's most priceless commodities – its lumber.

We had bought fruits and bread in the town and were pleasantly surprised that our ticket included two meals, served at one end of the deck. The food was basic beans, rice and fried fish but it tasted delicious to us. We even tried alligator meat for the first time and it tasted delicious too. The communal bathroom, at the back of the barge, was a row of sinks attached to the wall and, when you turned around, you had the most magnificent view of the Amazon River.

We slept on the deck in our hammocks with probably thirty or so other travelers. I stretched out next to a young Indian woman and her baby. I didn't hear that baby cry once – she was content to just rock next to her mom. I don't think I have slept anywhere as comfortable as on that river barge, swinging in that hammock while the jungle passed by.

Tour guides always warn of drinking the water in these remote places. At the dock, I had watched as hoses filled water tanks on the roof of the barge, which made me feel confident. However, halfway through the trip the water ran out and I noticed hoses being thrown into the river and water being pumped into these same tanks. We heeded those guide warnings after that. But I always say that if Gert and I didn't get some life-threatening disease from our travels, we would probably live forever.

The barge pulled into landings along the river to load and unload people and their wares. At each stop, people from the settlements rushed on board carrying food they had made to be sold. The atmosphere was of one big chaotic scene but it seemed to work. We even bought food ourselves, smoked alligator meat and I must admit it tasted delicious even though I tried to avoid meat these days.

We got talking to an English-speaking gentleman from the rainforest who was returning to visit family. He lived in Lima with his Canadian wife and had worked for most of his life in the oil fields. We spent an enjoyable afternoon discussing politics and how Peru's natural resources were being exploited by other countries. The lumber and oil exports thrived but left the country poorer than ever.

⌇

When I look back on that time I realize how fortunate I was to experience this part of South America. It seems like a dream to me now as I sit at my computer in the middle of Long Island, New York – one of the most consumer-crazy environments in the United States. I will never forget the beauty of this area or the kindness of these people during this part of our five-year journey.

20

GALAPAGOS

My niece, Vanessa, had asked right from the start of our trip if she could join us for a week in the Galapagos Islands. Vanessa is a science teacher and Galapagos is a science teacher's dream. In recent years, the isolation of this group of islands allows creatures to live without worrying about humans coming to hunt and kill them.

I warned Vanessa it would be crowded on board but if she didn't mind that, we didn't either. We cleared a spot in the v-berth, the forward part of the boat and she slept there squashed between her bags. Fortunately, as a seasoned traveler, she knows how to travel light.

I had told her nothing about Gigi or Adrian but I didn't need to; she got the picture within the first two days. Gigi's annoying maniacal laughter was probably what tipped her off. "How has Uncle Gert put up with her so long?" Vanessa asked, knowing Gert's famed impatience.

Vanessa had researched things she wanted to do and at the top of her list was a horse ride to the top of one of the many volcanoes. Now, I'm not a horse person. I admire them for their grace and beauty, but sitting in a saddle for hours is not my favorite form of transport. I've fallen from horses before but I decided to be a sport and join Vanessa on a tour.

Of course, Gigi insisted on coming too, being the horsewoman she claimed she was. On the steep ride up a narrow pass to the top of the volcano, her cackles of laughter did nothing to calm my nerves. When she rode her horse too close to mine I was terrified she would knock me over the steep edge. Was I being paranoid?

At the top at last, I thankfully dismounted to ease my sore butt. As the tour guide began his talk, no doubt fascinating and informative, I did some deep breathing and wandered off alone to get back into the Zen of the moment. I stared out over the awesome beauty, the 360-degree view of the Pacific Ocean, and the volcano itself – grey and rugged rocks like the surface of the moon.

But my mind was elsewhere. Vanessa's presence had reminded me of home news I was trying to deal with, like the cancer my elder sister was struggling with. Strolling alone on the gritty black path I spotted an unlikely burst of color – a flower growing between some rocks. I marveled at the way it had sprouted, here in all this barren grayness. A thought came into my mind, a saying of my mother's: '*In the darkest of times there is always hope.*' I hang on to these words in times of despair and this seemed like one of those moments.

The guide was calling, the tour was over. We remounted the horses for the downward trek which looked twice as steep from up here. My horse, delighted to be heading homeward, quickened his pace and deepened my fear of falling. His bouncing and pounding punished my sore butt. I slept on my side for the next two nights.

As we walked back to the boat, Vanessa grabbed my arm. "Is Uncle Gert cooking tonight? No offense but Gigi's cooking leaves a lot to be desired."

Part of the deal with Gigi and Adrian had been that Gigi

would do the cooking. The galley had become her domain. I told Vanessa to leave it to me.

Yes, Gert did cook dinner that night, and for the next two evenings Vanessa treated us to dinner at a restaurant on the island. Problem solved. We ate well and Gigi, I'm sure, enjoyed the break.

We took boat tours to see the sea lions and the two foot tall penguins in their natural environment. We were allowed to go ashore but warned not touch them. And of course, we made a special trip to meet Lonesome George, the world's oldest giant tortoise. The last survivor of the Pinta species, he was considered one of the rarest creatures in the world and at least a hundred years old when he died in 2012, six years after we had seen him. His relatives had been exterminated by whalers and seal hunters, so he was wary of people. I looked at him and thought: *If I were you, George, I'd be suspicious too.* Attempts to encourage him to mate had failed so when he died, that was it. It makes you wonder about nature.

Between tours Vanessa swam but no amount of persuasion would get me in that cold water. I don't know why the temperature surprised me. I guess I just imagined the Pacific would be warm. It's art I teach, not science.

The days went by too quickly. I was glad, when the time came, that Vanessa and I would be traveling back to the U.S. together. She would help me to take my mind off things. Gert and I had been talking. We both knew that, after he had crossed the Pacific I would have to make the Big Decision. I would not be flying back and forth anymore. With that great distance between us, we just couldn't afford the flights.

During the day, while they were crossing the Pacific, I was in Buffalo and too caught up in the antics of teenagers with behavioral problems to give them much thought. It was only in the evening when I returned to the little apartment I had rented that I questioned my staying behind. Thank God Maggie May understood me. I could tell from those mournful eyes what she was thinking: *She* was the smart one. *She* had known, right from *Zivio*'s maiden voyage, that she was not going any further.

They made the crossing in twenty-eight days keeping me informed of their progress via SailMail, a radio-based email system that boaters use when they don't have line of sight radio links to the internet. Thank heavens for this and so many of the other communication methods we now take for granted.

The sailing was uneventful, Gert reported, and at one point, out of sheer boredom, they even jumped in the ocean to swim. But he wasn't telling me everything.

Although nothing had been said in the emails, I would learn later that morale had deteriorated on board. Gigi had been behaving strangely, even before they left. Part of the deal was that she did the housekeeping but one day she had just taken to her bunk and slept, or pretended to sleep, for days. Gert had serious thoughts about whether or not she should undertake the crossing.

"What the hell is going on?" he asked Adrian, in his usual delicate way. "I'm not crossing the Pacific with that kind of bullshit."

Adrian apologized and confessed this wasn't the first time she had withdrawn like that. I never got the full story and I'm sure much was lost in the translation, but I had kind of suspected she had something diagnosable. (Gert thinks I read too much into people. His summary of anyone with odd behavior is 'Jerk,' though he expresses his opinion more colorfully).

After Gert's little speech, even Adrian thought maybe Gigi should not travel with them, but said he would talk to her.

"Suddenly she was up," Gert said, "cleaning, cooking, and laughing like nothing had happened."

But during the journey she was either up or down emotionally, Gert said, and at one point, mid Pacific, she tossed his most precious possessions overboard – the 'special' tobacco he kept in a plastic pouch in the cockpit.

There was no easy solution here; they were in the middle of the Pacific Ocean and Gert certainly couldn't throw *her* overboard – though I think, if I had been on board, I might have been tempted.

I did not know about this incident until after the crossing, I might have been more concerned about it if I had. Other than her manic laughter it was hard to get a take on what Gigi was really like – smart? dumb? I didn't know. Certainly when, back in South America, she'd had her nipples pierced and a gold string strung between them, I had realized we had little in common.

Gert too, had been perplexed at the time. "What good are they for except hanging Christmas ornaments on?" he wanted to know.

I was nevertheless impressed by any woman sailing across that ocean. It is not an easy undertaking. I only knew I could never have taken more than a couple of days living on board with Gigi.

I'm sure the mood for the rest of the trip was frosty, and Gert wasn't surprised when Adrian told him they found another boat to crew on.

Knowing I was soon to join him, Gert was not concerned. But even if I was not due to return, as I know my husband, he would have sailed on alone, no matter what. Brave, or pig-headed?

By the time I arrived in Tahiti, Adrian and Gigi had transferred to the other boat with all their gear and Gert was alone on *Zivio* again. He told me there were no hard feelings between them, from the little I knew of Gigi, I didn't believe that. She looked to me like she could be pretty vindictive.

But there's a twist to this story.

The next morning, I awoke to someone knocking on our hull.

"*Bonjour, bonjour* Carolina, welcome to Tahiti," Gigi's voice called out.

So much for the peaceful island paradise I had been dreaming of. I wanted to pull the sheet up over my head but Gert just rolled his eyes and told them to come on board.

They had just spent their first night aboard their next boat. "*Mon Dieu*, eet eez like 'ell," Gigi wailed, "roaches everywhere, and green stuff growing on everysing!"

I was unsurprised. The owner, Captain Bill as he was known, was living the wild and crazy life of a sailor for whom housekeeping was not a priority. The boat had been trashed by Hurricane Katrina and he had bought it cheaply. Captain Bill was quite the party man who enjoyed his drink. His previous crew had jumped ship but that is not unusual; the average life expectancy of any crew is two years. Tight spaces don't make for great bedfellows.

Gigi complained on and on about the 'feelzy' boat – comparing it to the 'perfect *Zeevio*' but Adrian insisted it was seaworthy and moreover, going in the right direction.

We didn't feel bad about their leaving. We had always known their goal was Australia while our direction was west. This was the perfect time, in more ways than one, for us to go our separate ways.

⁓

In Papeete Harbor, Tahiti, we could hardly find a place to anchor and were crammed in along with fifty or so other boats. Papeete was a big disappointment. The harbor itself is filthy, and crowded with cruise ships and cruising boats like ours, which from here would turn south for destinations like Australia and New Zealand or west towards the Far East.

I was already feeling down. The first thing I had done after landing in Tahiti was to call my sister. Maggie May had contracted a kidney problem two days before my flight out and was being treated. The vet feared the outcome as this problem was common with aging Golden Retrievers. I felt sick with worry. I had talked with my sister about what would be done if Maggie May's condition deteriorated. My heart was breaking and the impact of all this traveling was starting to sink in. Maggie May died just days after we set sail from Tahiti. It was a sad time for Gert and me and we vowed never, ever, to have another pet until we settled down in one place.

We rowed ashore to explore. There was nothing quaint about the Papeete waterfront. The anonymous grey buildings added nothing to the tropical island spirit. "Where are the grass skirts and tiki bars?" I grumbled. With its expensive stores, all selling the same trinkets, this looked just like every other tourist trap.

Shopping appeared to be the primary goal of most of the people we saw strolling the streets. Almost all the merchandise had to be imported; carrots in the grocery stores sold for eight dollars apiece.

We glanced at the menus of some of the restaurants and decided we must have made a wrong turn – these were New York prices, way too high for us. We ate fast food from the trucks instead, fish sandwiches and fried bananas and ceviche prepared with the added delight of coconut juice. I had never eaten them that way but they tasted pretty good. Fish was plentiful but still not cheap to buy. Luckily, we still had a tuna we caught on the last stretch which would keep fresh for two or three days in our freezer box.

Many French people lived on the island, I learned, teachers and municipal workers making the same wages they made in France and that is why prices were so high. But from what I could see, people in the scruffy back streets lived in comparative poverty. *How did these people manage?* I wondered.

"Beware of the pickpockets," people warned us.

~

There was nothing to keep us in this harbor. We hauled anchor and sailed to the opposite side of the island and I'm so glad we did. Here at last was the Tahiti that Marlon Brando had fallen in love with. Lush, hilly scenery. Quaint little homes painted in brilliant pinks and blues and greens, each with a garden in front filled with tropical fruits – guava, passion fruit, and papaya all growing wild. Yes, this was the island I was looking for. We docked in a quiet cove and rowed ashore.

In a small, hut-style restaurant we ate delicious ocean fish in a mango sauce. This, I was sure, was paradise. I've often tried to copy that recipe but it never comes out the same. I think the ingredient of the island atmosphere – eating outside with a view of turquoise waters sparkling like diamonds in the tropical sunshine – made it taste so good.

One night, back in the harbor, Captain Bill invited us to join him in a waterfront bar where he was getting his first tattoo and wanted to celebrate with friends. Tattooing is an art form in the islands and many of the natives are covered with bright colorful images.

We rowed to the bar and there sat Bill.

"Hey, pull up a chair," he bellowed. He'd obviously taken someone's advice and was anesthetizing himself with whisky for the procedure. At least a dozen shot glasses of alcohol sat empty on the table.

Bill had hired a local tattoo artist. "Here he comes," he announced and in waddled a very stocky native, shirtless and in shorts and tattoos over his entire body. He put down his black leather case and proceeded to unpack his vials of ink and needles and arrange them on the sticky tabletop.

"Doesn't look real sanitary to me," I whispered to Gert.

"It's ok, I think that bottle says 'alcohol'," Gert said.

"Yeah. Except it's not *rubbing* alcohol."

Well, the night wore on with more shots and more tattooing but after a few hours Bill sprang up as he couldn't take the pain.

The tattoo looked pretty good but if you ever meet a sailboat captain with an unfinished parrot on his shoulder you'll know who it is.

There's yet another twist to this story. Captain Bill had to abandon ship and return home for treatment. Adrian and Gigi were left to deliver the boat to Australia on their own.

We spent a couple more uncomfortable days rockin' and rollin' in the harbor of Papeete before continuing northwest to the island of Bora Bora.

This gorgeous place is surrounded by a barrier reef and a lagoon with crystal turquoise water. In the center of the island, two peaks rise – Mount Pahia and Mount Otemanu, remnants of an extinct volcano, I read. I sighed over the lushness and beauty of this island. No wonder Marlon Brando had chosen it as a location for Mutiny on the Bounty.

We rowed ashore to explore a picturesque village. The locals lived in pretty little huts with thatched roofs, from where they sold fresh fruit and fish. There were fewer signs of tourism here, and an absence of expensive restaurants and boutiques. The mood was low-key; people strolled or sat in the shade, chatting, making flower garlands. Of course, the island may now have changed as nothing stays the same, but back then it was idyllic. I savored those lazy days, especially as I knew what was coming up next – a six day crossing with one of us constantly at the wheel. Every minute of every night and day.

Gert must have sensed what I was thinking. "We'll look into

that self-steering equipment when we get to Samoa," he announced.

I narrowed my eyes at him. "Is that a *promise?*"

On the first night out we were again struck by a rogue wave. Rogue waves are defined in Webster's as waves twice the significant wave height of the area. Some can, and have, knocked boats on their side or even sunk large ships. In short, they're scary as hell and I didn't need a dictionary to tell me that. This one tossed me from my bunk and against the door of the head. I thought my nose was broken, that I was going to black out, but I tried not to scream bloody murder and add to the pandemonium. The boat rocked madly, pots and pans and books tumbled from the shelves. Some of the Pacific had found its way down below, mingling with my blood.

When Gert had got *Zivio* back under control, he yelled down: "Are you alright?"

I clutched an icepack to my nose and bit back the 'F' word. The icepack did not prevent two black circles forming around my eyes. I looked into the mirror later and a raccoon gaped back at me.

22

SUVAROV

On the sail to Suvarov, a journey we estimated as a week, something strange happened during the night that I will always remember. I was steering while Gert was sleeping below. Suddenly, as I stood alone in the cockpit, with only a sliver of moon for company, a huge dark mass appeared off to my port side and worse, it was moving straight towards the boat.

Not another rogue wave! I thought in a panic. I opened my mouth to scream but my throat was paralyzed. *The mass would surely smash into the boat*, I thought, bracing myself for death; by now you know me well enough to know that I am always bracing for death.

But the dark shape slipped right under the boat and emerged on the opposite side. *A whale?* I gripped the wheel harder. *Zivio would be flipped on its side like a matchbox!* But after the mass had passed, *Zivio* was still upright and I was still on board. I relaxed my grip and breathed again. I had only felt a gentle movement, like a whisper, soft and in a strange way comforting. What had it been?

I stared intently into the inky sea. Slowly I realized I was looking at a pod of dolphins. I could just make out some shapes near the surface as they circled back and played around the boat, jumping in the air, swimming next to *Zivio* as if trying to out-race her. I laughed out loud, from joy and relief.

I took this sighting as another sign, you know how big I am on 'signs'. Dolphins, I decided, were good luck omens plus there is nothing that can lift your spirits more than dolphins playing. A warm glow passed through me. I decided this visitation was my own personal memorial service to Maggie May. I was sure her spirit was with those dolphins, they are such happy creatures, just as she had been. To this day, when I see dolphins I think of my much-missed Maggie.

It was nighttime when we spotted Suvarov. This tiny island, dwarfed by the Pacific, is also known, confusingly, as Suvarrow, Suvaro, and Suvaru. Take your pick.

It amazed me how we could find such a speck of an island in all that ocean; not that I didn't have confidence in our navigating skills – we had maps installed in our computer by this point and I did 'kind of' know what I was looking at most of the time. I blame my father for my poor navigation skills. Back on the farm, whenever he sent me somewhere to pick up parts for a tractor or truck and I couldn't figure out where the place was, his solution was always: "*Ask*, girl. That's what gas stations are for." Well, there were no gas stations in the middle of the Pacific.

We preferred not to chance entering the harbor, deciding instead to sail back and forth outside until daylight as the chartbook suggested. I felt miserable. Waves had been breaking over the deck all night and we were constantly soaked but at least the water was warm and land was in sight. The waves were steep, although if you'd asked Gert he'd insist they were never more than three or four feet, tops. Gert says this about every wave height – I triple his estimation. In any case I'm sure I looked pathetic, completely soaked and deadly tired. Without self-steering, one of us had to be constantly at the wheel and I felt the dawn would never break.

The island has an interesting history from what little I had read about it. It seems it was discovered by a ship that was following a flock of birds, and reportedly named after a Russian general (Suvarov – the name of that ship). And although it was not *the* Treasure Island of the book, it deserved to have that name. In the nineteenth century an old chest had been found containing gold and silver valued at five million dollars at today's value. The story goes that, while digging a place to lay her eggs, a turtle had unearthed the chest. A New Zealander, Henry Mair, then found the chest and because it was too heavy to carry back to his boat he buried it, carefully noting its position. He planned to come back for it later but as fate would have it, old Henry was clubbed to death by natives in the New Hebrides and knowledge of the secret hiding place died with him. Easy come, easy go.

A golden dawn broke and we entered the harbor. *Zivio* was quickly recognized. Sailors we had met along the way, some from as far back as Grenada, called out and waved. It filled me with joy to see familiar boats and faces. We had all come so far but we were starting to feel more like a community, a happy family regrouping. We all had something in common. There aren't too many people who sail around the world.

We anchored and rowed straight over to our friends' boat for champagne; any safe crossing deserves a celebration. They laughed at my eyes which now had blue and black rings around them from my encounter with the head door. They teased me saying I must have been yelling at Gert the whole way about our lack of self-steering, and he in turn had popped me on the nose. (Which, by the way would have never happened – Gert would have finished up overboard, however far from land we were).

About ten boats were anchored while we were there, some we knew, some we didn't, but as sailors do in these circumstances, everyone bonded quickly. In the evening we made barbecues on the beach, all donating something to the meals which became minor feasts. As we ate and drank, everyone compared notes – where they had been, what adventures they'd had, where their next port would be. Sailors love to tell stories and some of these, I'm sure, fell into the B.S. category. Either that or we had been sailing in different parts of the world.

Suvarov has an area of just over three and a half square miles. At the time we were there, it was inhabited by only four people – a couple and their two young boys. The couple served as caretakers and customs officials. Suvarov has the loosest customs office I had ever been in, but they gave us the official stamp and that is all we needed. It seemed like the perfect 'summer job' to me, if indeed it *was* summer. With all this travel, I felt season-less.

The boys were probably eleven or twelve years old and were, I suspect, home schooled by their parents during this time. Sun and sea – I can't imagine a better education. The boys looked like characters out of Tom Sawyer, a coming-of-age book set in the rural south of the United States. They were as brown as berries, shirtless and shoeless most of the time, with the wide smiles I saw so often in the faces of the Polynesians. Their lives were so free and active. If they had been brought up in America their parents would have them fitted out in helmets and knee pads and sprayed them with toxic anti-bug juice. They'd be walking around and staring into their cell phones. These kids, instead, were fascinated by the sailors who came in, curious about where they were from and what it was like living in those countries, the USA, France, England. They would tag on behind us, pointing out different birds, of which there were plenty, and even bringing us a giant coconut crab for one of our nightly barbecues.

For an island seemingly in the middle of the Pacific, I was amazed at the biodiversity – a word I had learned from my niece Vanessa. There were sea turtles and whales (which unfortunately we didn't see – not in that area anyway). The island also has hundreds of birds that we had never seen before. It was home to at least eleven species of seabirds. Don't hold me to that number – I read it in the guidebook. The atoll supports (I also read) significant colonies of 'red, masked and brown booby birds' whatever they are, and is home to species of 'frigate' birds which, I was to learn, are tropical seabirds known for being particularly aggressive and stealing food from other birds. I guess if I lived in the middle of the Pacific I would become food-aggressive too – I mean who knows where your next meal is coming from?

The island at that time, was also home to thousands of huge and tasty coconut crabs, by now probably nearing extinction. And sharks! The ones we saw in the harbor were smallish but I was sure that every once in a while a relative of Jaws would swim in, just to check out the local human-menu.

We gave the caretakers, I wish I could remember their names, a can of gas when they ran out. We had no need of it anyway as by now our dinghy motor had broken. What else is new? The caretaker took Gert fishing in the harbor entrance, the best fishing place according to him, and sure enough Gert caught a tuna there by just trolling a line off the back of their dinghy. We shared the tuna with him and saved the rest for the evening barbecue. These days, years later, I can't eat fish without remembering how different really fresh fish tastes.

We spent a few days walking around the small island The boys followed us everywhere, self-appointed guides. They speared fish and showed us how to catch the coconut crabs. Later I rowed Gert around the harbor as he wanted to try his hand at spearing a fish, like the boys had done. How hard could it be? While he snorkeled, searching for fish, I rowed close beside him. All of a sudden I spotted a fin in the water and it was coming straight towards our dinghy. I screeched *"Shark!"* and Gert, after a quick glance behind him, scrambled back on board faster than I'd ever seen him move.

The fin turned out to belong to a small nurse shark but to me, a shark is a shark. Gert was not tempted to return to the water. He never speared a fish either.

Suvarov is a special respite for sailors before they sail across the Pacific but our community of friends was growing smaller by the day. Among boaters a closeness develops quickly which you don't get on land. We knew we would all be going our separate ways soon and, since no-one was going to Samoa, our next landing, I realized sadly that most of us might never meet again.

I always felt that I was the least experienced of the women sailors we had met. Especially compared to the woman from California we had met in Tahiti. She and her husband had been sailing since their early twenties and had raised their two sons on board. The romantic side of me thought this was wonderful but could I have done it? I'm honestly not sure. Living aboard can be rough, especially if your budget is as small as ours. Perhaps some people thought the way we traveled, on a wooden boat and without self-steering, was romantic.

Everyone has a different reason for sailing, I couldn't help noticing how many old men were sailing with women less than half their age. I could only guess the young girls were looking for adventure and hey, to tell their friends they were on a sailboat. And I don't think it needs explaining why the old men took the young women along. *Wow* – is that sexist?

Even of the 'normal' couples we met, the husbands were usually on their second or third marriages. Then there are those couples, like Gert and me, who are both happily married and truly looking for adventure. For us, though, this was not a life-choice but a brief adventure. We had made the promise that after five years we would stop. Sailing is a tough life and long-distance sailing can be particularly difficult. I knew I didn't have the stomach for a lifetime of it.

Time was getting short and we would soon leave Suvarov. As we sailed out of the harbor, the only ones heading for Samoa, I felt as if I was leaving my land roots. That I was truly living a life as different as I could ever have imagined. We were a long way away from that pond in Lockport, New York.

23

SAMOA

After another six-day sail we arrived in American Samoa; a series of five main islands and two coral atolls. The islands are home to, what else? U.S. bases. The Pele Army Reserve Center is located here and the U.S. Marine Corps recruiting station is on Nu'uuli, another of the islands. American Samoa – not to be confused with Samoa – is considered an unincorporated territory of the U.S.

We headed for the main island, Tutuila, to provision and prepare for the next big sail. The cyclone season was approaching so we didn't have time to waste. Our plan was to sail north of the equator towards Kiribati, but it didn't turn out that way. *The best laid plans of mice and men,* as they say.

This was a working harbor, and not very picturesque. Garbage and debris floated in the dirty water. As we'd motored past Charlie Tuna's factory we were hit by the stench of, well, tuna, the island's chief export. The factory, built on one side of the harbor, looked like every other big, dirty warehouse. Commercial ships tied alongside ready for loading. Oil and fuel spills floated on the greasy-looking water. We wouldn't be jumping off for a swim any time soon.

High hills surround the harbor so at least we were protected from the winds we had just experienced coming from Suvarov. The harbor was packed with boats of all sizes and shapes. With so little space to maneuver we had to be extra careful about where to drop our anchor as this situation was prime for snagged anchors and boats dragging into each other. I hoped our stay would be short.

We inched our way into an anchorage that was so packed we would need to tie up to another sailboat in order to go ashore for custom clearing formalities. We called out for permission to anchor alongside a steel boat that was flying the Turkish flag, red with a white moon and star. The captain looked a little grumpy and mumbled a reluctant "ok", but his girlfriend eagerly waved us over. She was holding a cat and seemed delighted to strike up a conversation – in fact she looked starved for company.

Gert was keen to know about their boat. The captain, Kerem, had built it himself out of steel with the sole intention of sailing around the world. He had no interest in sightseeing, he told us. Being very determined, he had given himself three years and was well on his way to achieving that goal. He had left from Turkey, crossed both the Atlantic and Pacific oceans, and now had one year to go.

Being non-competitive, I didn't see any point in non-stop sailing and fortunately neither did Gert. We hadn't undertaken our own journey to prove anything. Gert always said he would have preferred to drive a car around the world if that were possible, and that would have been my preference too. The goal of our journeys was to see for ourselves all those places I had read about in National Geographic, to meet other people, to experience other cultures.

Turkan, the captain's girlfriend, was friendly and easy to like. It took a little longer to warm up to Kerem himself. He had been to the U.S. to study and hated it. "Americans are loud and brash and know nothing of the world!" he would say. Admittedly, and unfortunately, some of that is true. (Gert, being Danish, was exempt from his blunt pronouncements of course).

But what do you know? After this inauspicious beginning, Kerem and Turkan were eventually to become our dearest friends. Turkan was very different to Karem. She worked as an interpreter and writer for a publication out of Turkey. She had visited the U.S. – well, New York City anyway – and absolutely enjoyed it.

Years later Gert would crew on their boat from Yemen, up the Red Sea, through the Suez Canal to their home port in Turkey. I would fly to Istanbul from where we would take their boat cruising through the Mediterranean. But that's another story.

We had been sailing now close to five years. Time was flying and so was our money. *Zivio* was starting to have mechanical problems, understandable in a boat of her age. Gert went down to check over the engine as it wasn't running as smooth as he'd liked. He emerged later, covered in grease. "Looks like we're going to be here longer than expected," he announced. "She needs a valve job."

Great, I thought. I had hoped for a simple oil change "And how long is that going to take?"

"Depends on how quickly we can find a supplier and how fast they can ship."

All I could think of was the cyclone season approaching. I was not feeling good.

We rowed ashore to look for the local post office from where we could call the U.S. to locate the necessary parts. After what seemed like the hundredth call, Gert found a supplier on the East Coast.

"They'll be here in no time," Gert said as we rowed back to the boat.

I knew what that meant. The shipping costs would be out of sight. Gert knew what I was thinking; we had allotted just so much money for this trip and it did not include expensive repairs.

We had already talked about the sails. They were showing signs of wear and tear. They had never been replaced and were already old when we bought *Zivio*. We had talked about buying new ones in the Far East where everyone said they were cheaper. But would the old ones get us there?

The good thing about being stuck was that it gave us time to explore. Buses traveled almost everywhere and we rode them to see what the island looked like away from the anchorage. The rainforest, gorges, and waterfalls were a wonderful surprise.

Samoa was never intended to be more than a jump off to the Far East for us. Now that it was turning out to be a longer stop, I wish I had read up more of the local culture.

It was here that I saw my first real live Sumo wrestler, or should I say, many of them; never have I seen so many obese people, male and female. Obesity seems to be accepted in the Samoan culture, even desired among women, but it was still a shock to me, coming from NYC as I did, where people look anorexic and wear black all the time. Outside a local church one day, we watched a bridal party unload from their vehicles; each person had to be well over two hundred pounds.

I found the Samoan culture fascinating. Before visiting the island, I had heard of the existence of the Fa'afafine but knew little more about them. These are the Samoan men raised as girls and considered a third gender. They are primarily heterosexual, and accepted as part of the Samoan culture and not ridiculed as LGBT persons in other places often are. We have a lot to learn from other cultures.

We had seen some at a music and dance festival where traditional Samoan dancers performed. That evening ended with a pork barbecue; the slaughtered pig had been buried in sand and covered with seaweed for more than a day. I am no longer a meat eater but I remember that pork as being delicious.

We even took a tour of the Sunkist Tuna Factory. It looked run down and dirty to me.

～

The year 2007 was almost upon us. Our five-year mark was coming up, the cyclone season was rapidly closing in and we were getting nervous. Our parts had not arrived. Gert had already taken the motor apart in readiness. As our engine was located midship and accessed through the companionway between the front and back cabin, grease and oil smells hung everywhere. But the waiting time was not completely wasted – Gert, as promised, had bought and attached self-steering windvane. At last!

When not exploring, we passed the time chatting with other boaters until the late evening. With Kerem and Turkan – the atheist and the non-practicing Muslim – we drank ouzo, the Middle East equivalent of Danish Aquavit. The Turks, we learned, didn't pour shots as you do with Aquavit but knocked it back by the glassful.

We talked politics. The times were changing and the thought of Bush years finally being over was a relief. Yeah! We argued, primarily about the U.S. involvement in the Middle East. Often, we were invited by a young French couple, Jean and Monique, who were traveling in a very small sailboat. There was hardly room in their boat to turn around but the most exquisite food appeared from that tiny French galley. They had been working on a pearl farm in French Polynesia – didn't I tell you sailors were interesting people?

I was full of admiration for that incredible Frenchwoman. She canned everything from fish to seaweed. She also maintained their boat, it seemed, as her husband enjoyed socializing more than working.

Our parts finally arrived from the States. Half of them were wrong and so, after repacking and sending them back again, we anxiously awaited the right ones. It was now October 2006 and yes, the cyclone season was officially here.

We had hoped to sail in tandem with the Turkish boat. The goal was to head north to get out of the cyclone zone. Knowing that the weather would only get worse the longer they stayed in American Samoa, Kerem and Turkan decided to leave before us. We planned to meet on the island of Kiribati, north of the equator.

I watched sadly as they sailed out of the harbor, comforted only by the fact we would soon meet up again.

Or so I thought.

The right parts arrived and *Zivio* was quickly ready to sail. I felt buoyant as we motored out of the harbor with me at the helm and Gert preparing to raise a sail. All of a sudden the engine stopped. *Zivio* would go neither forward nor in reverse. When she started drifting slowly towards the Sunkist Tuna Factory, we both felt slightly sick. Perilously close to the docks and other boats, we threw out an anchor until a fishing boat noticed our dilemma and towed us back to the anchorage.

Once we were safely anchored, Gert dropped below to figure out what the trouble was. A part connecting the engine to the transmission had broken. It took him a couple of days to fix it and we were off again. This time I was feeling less than confident and very worried – what else would go wrong? And how would we now survive financially? These last repairs had depleted most of our savings and we still had to buy new sails. We would now be living entirely on my little pension so if anything happened, that would be *it*. I said nothing of my fears to Gert. I didn't need to. He had been married long enough to me to know what I was thinking.

We were heading north west towards the non-American Samoa. We'd had no radio contact from Kerem and Turkan, but

I found it comforting to know they were somewhere out there ahead of us. The winds were fickle, sometimes gusting, sometimes calm. I quickly learned that a windvane relying on wind does not work well – if at all – in such conditions so we were back to manual steering. The first day out was just solid hours of motoring. The next day was not much better but at times we could use the sail, albeit in a strong wind that rolled *Zivio* up on one side to a scary angle. I felt exhausted and depressed and increasingly worried about the days ahead – before we reached the equator, the weather might do anything.

The second night we were hit by torrential rain and high winds. Motoring was difficult and somewhere after midnight, as I steered, staring out into the night, Gert noticed our storm sail was ripping. Hanging on tightly, he moved forward to pull it down. Waves were crashing from all different directions and we were both soaked. I gripped the wheel tightly and prayed.

The sun rose brilliantly the next day and the calm sea sparkled. As Gert sailed, I sat down next to him and announced, "I will not go any further. I am not sailing around the world, soaking wet, at five miles an hour."

There. I had said it.

Gert was half expecting this, I'm sure, but he tried to convince me. "But we have so much more to see!"

"No," I insisted. "We said five years and the five years are up."

Gert pleaded. "Do you know how great you'll feel once we've completed a circumnavigation?"

"I don't care," I wailed. "I can accomplish a lot and not risk my life." I surprised myself that I wasn't blubbering when I said all this.

"But it will get better…" he argued.

I couldn't listen. I wanted off. "If you want to continue," I told him, "you'll have to find your own crew. For sure it will not be me."

I suppose there was hatred in the air at that point – he hated me for giving up and I hated him for being such a hard head. It could have been a turning point in our marriage. I would have gone back alone and, I almost thought, Gert would go on without me.

After back and forth bickering for the rest of the day, Gert finally gave in. The time was up, he knew it too. He didn't want to sail with strangers again and sailing alone didn't appeal to him.

So, we turned *Zivio* around and sailed back to American Samoa.

We were both sick with disappointment and hardly spoke. If the weather had continued to be kind, I like to think I would have changed my mind and pushed on. But that is hindsight speaking.

I've said it before – one of Gert's best attributes is acceptance. Once a decision has been made he does not hold a grudge, he goes on to the next step. We just had not decided what the next step would be.

"Well," he sighed, "we're not sailing back to the States, and we're not abandoning *Zivio* here, so we'll have to sell."

Sell a wooden boat in the South Pacific? I didn't see a big market out here.

~

We dropped anchor again in American Samoa. Within the hour Monique and Jean had rowed over, bursting with curiosity.

"What happened?" Monique asked.

"That's it," Gert calmly said. "*Zivio* is up for sale."

Jean opened his eyes wide. "We'll buy her!" he said.

I couldn't believe how quickly things were happening – we hadn't even set a price.

"She's yours for five thousand," Gert announced.

~

When they left, eyes aglow, to row back to their boat, I glared at Gert as if he were crazy. "Five thousand dollars – you *know* she is worth more than that!"

He sighed. "Look, I see it this way. We've had five years. *Zivio* owes us nothing. We've sailed almost halfway around the world in our own home, rent free, and now it's time to move on."

I knew it in my heart, he was right.

So, just like that, it was over. We all met the next day and sealed the deal.

We were going home.

～

Rowing out of that harbor with our few belongings was sad and I confess I held back some tears. Did I feel I had given up? I suppose I did, but as our buddy in Grenada used to say: "A man's gotta do what a man's gotta do".

I guess that went for women too.

24

RETURN

Within two weeks we were on a plane to the U.S. still trying to come to terms with this finality. The plane stopped off in Hawaii, the cheapest route I could find. We arrived early in the morning at the Honolulu International Airport on Oahu, one of Hawaii's five islands.

With a one night layover, we decided to find a cheap youth hostel and then tour some of the island. I use the term 'youth hostel' loosely – we were sixty years old at the time but had learned from experience that all ages seem to be welcome. I left Gert in charge of our luggage in an airport coffee shop while I took my handy Lonely Planet guide to a pay phone. I located a youth hostel nearby but no one was answering at that time of the morning.

As I made my way back to the coffee shop, I chuckled to see Gert at a table in deep conversation with Santa's little helper – a woman in a long red sparkly dress with white fur on the collar and cuffs. To complete the look she wore an elf's hat dangling a big white puffball. *Boy,* I thought, *he can find them!*

"I heard about you having to sell your boat," she said. With a sad smile and in a slow Texan drawl, she told us she had just put her daughter on a flight back to one of the other islands.

More chatting revealed she had an apartment in town, just two blocks off the beach, and this led us to ditching the youth hostel idea and renting her spare room for the night. Hotels in that area were charging upwards of $500 a night, but she asked only $50. I think she was lonely and hey, it was Christmas. We followed her to her Jeep.

Gert and I have always been lucky in the people we have met and Linda, the Texas lady, was no exception. Before taking us back to her apartment, she gave us a short tour of the Waikiki Beach area and showed us where to pick up a tour bus that would drive us around the perimeter of Oahu.

Our room was separate from the apartment she shared with her husband, and even had its own bathroom. After a quick shower, we hurried into the town to catch the tour bus, a hop-on, hop-off service to allow passengers to tour the sites at their own pace. Gert and I opted to get off on the northern coast of Oahu first as this is a world-famous surfing area. Not that either of us surfed but it is one sport I have always enjoyed watching. I told Gert I was sure I had been a world-class surfer in some other life. He just rolls his eyes to comments like these as I've claimed to have various identities in past lives.

The Waimea Beach was crowded with surfers. The waves were exceptionally high that day, some reaching thirty feet, we learned. This was not an area for amateurs. I imagined how sailing in waves like those would have been, and almost felt sick. Thank goodness I would never know now. We grabbed some drinks from an outside bar, sat on the beach and watched the surfing in complete awe. After an hour or so we dragged ourselves off to the bus stop.

The tour buses circle the island; an entire tour takes a full day and we had to get going if we didn't want to miss anything. The bus driver announced we were nearing the Dole pineapple plantation and still had time to visit before the last stop of Pearl Harbor. We hopped off for a quick tour, but with time enough to plant a little pineapple. I wonder how big it is today.

The last stop was Pearl Harbor where a small launch took us to the USS Arizona Memorial. The Memorial is built over the site of the sunken wreckage of the massive battleship where over a thousand seamen lost their lives on December 7, 1941 in the surprise Japanese attack – the point where the United States entered WWII.

Funny, I had never wanted to visit Hawaii, considering it too touristy for me and far too expensive, but I found this a physically beautiful island, especially the north shore. Its part in the history of WWII made it an interesting side trip for us both. And we had made friends. Linda and husband Bob, also from Texas, kept in touch. For years after we exchanged Christmas cards.

The following day we took off for Los Angeles. As we started our descent the realization began to set in – we were back on land and boatless, with no jobs and no car. Moreover, Los Angeles is nearly three thousand miles away from New York. There was a lot to think about.

Michael, our adored 'son', met us at the airport, which definitely softened the blow of re-entry. He is always such a delight. He was living in Ojai in Northern California and told us we should stay with him and his girlfriend Jess for a while, in their little rented house in the Canyon.

California is such a beautiful state and I had often thought of living there when I was much younger. I wonder how different my life would have been had I traveled that road.

Michael told us he'd had to trash the VW bus we had given him five years earlier when we started out on our journey. It had rusted beyond repair but he had kept the engine which Gert, back then, had rebuilt. It was only right we should take it, Michael said. Moreover, he had just located the body of another VW camper...

Gert fitted the old motor into our 'new' bus. How strange that felt. After five years aboard *Zivio*, we were on land again and driving around in a vehicle that was, at least in part, the old Volkswagen bus that served us so well in the past. There has always been a VW bus in our lives and when we had started our long sail, giving it to Michael had seemed the right thing to do. Now, it appeared, the bus was coming back to us. *Hmmm.* Karma?

We tested it out by traveling down the California coast. There is nothing like touring the U.S. and camping. Prime ocean view for thirty-five dollars a night. We were looking forward to the cross-country trip home. By now I had located the cell phone that had flown with me into Tahiti. I hadn't connected it to international calling and never imagined it was still charged but surprise! It worked.

The first person I called was an old friend at the hospital where I had worked to ask if they knew of any social work jobs in the area. My old boss got on the line.

"Send me your resume," she said. "Someone has just quit and we need you!" Fate? Luck? I don't know what you'd call it.

Gert sat listening in amazement but by now he knew me well enough to realize I start planning right away. Gert rolls with the punches and once the decision had been made to sell *Zivio* – that was the hard part – it was just a matter of getting back to New York to make money.

To finance our next adventure?

≈

I called friends in North Carolina and told them we were back on dry land and making our way back to New York. "See you in a few weeks," I said.

Within a couple of days I received a call from them. They'd understood I couldn't live long without a dog and they knew of a golden retriever – one that, after many bad experiences, was looking for a good home. Her name was Maple May. Fate again?

We drove to Virginia to pick up our new baby. Her owners – the third set – did love her but Maple May wasn't the right dog for them. They were extremely disciplined and Maple May, it appeared, was not. Despite private trainers and dog school, Maple May still did whatever she wanted. We were soon to adopt the mantra 'it's Maple May's way or no way'. As the owner took us to the garage where the dog was kept, I eyed Gert who knew exactly what I was thinking: *Garage?* Our dogs had always lived inside our home, even slept in our beds. The owner was very organized; as we walked out of the door she handed us a booklet with 'all things Maple May', and when I asked if Maple really needed to be on a leash as we were only going a few feet to the car, she insisted Maple May "didn't really listen that well."

Maple May hopped willingly into the back of the bus. As we pulled out of the driveway I half expected her to turn around and howl for her past owner and home. Instead she curled up into my lap, snuggled into my arms and looked at me with the biggest, most expressive brown eyes I have ever seen. She was home. I sat with her like that, curled up and content, all the way back to Long Island.

Ending up where we started out. But, as they say, so much richer.

The End

AUTHOR'S NOTE

Thanks for purchasing and reading *Tacking Through Life*, I hope you enjoyed it.

A lot of people don't realize that the best way to help an author is to leave a review. So, if you had fun accompanying me on our voyage, please return to the site you purchased this book from and say a few words. It doesn't have to be long, just saying what you thought is fine and much appreciated. It also helps other readers make an informed decision about their purchases.

I love hearing from readers and authors alike, so if you'd like to stay in touch and be the first to know about forthcoming books and what I am up to, please visit me at:

www.sistershippress.com